MATHEMATICS

Louise Moore

Series Editor: **Richard Cooper**

RISING STARS

Rising Stars UK Ltd, 7 Hatchers Mews, Bermondsey Street, London SE1 3GS

www.risingstars-uk.com

All facts are correct at time of going to press.

First published 2003
Second edition 2008
Third edition 2010
This edition incorporating revisions 2014
Reprinted 2015

First edition written by: Richard Cooper
Illustrations: Tim Oliver and Clive Wakfer
Design: Clive Sutherland
Cover design: Burville-Riley Partnership

British Library Cataloguing in Publication Data
A CIP record for this book is available from the British Library.

ISBN 978-1-78339-417-3

Printed by Craft Print International Ltd., Singapore

Contents

How to use this book

What we have included:

- ★ Those topics at Level 3 that are trickiest to get right ('the tricky bits').
- ★ ALL Level 4 content so you know that you are covering all the topics that you need to understand in order to achieve Level 4.
- ★ A selection of our favourite test techniques, tips for revision and some advice on what the tests are all about, as well as the answers so you can see how you are getting on.

1. **Introduction** – This section tells you what you need to do to get a Level 4. It picks out the key learning objective and explains it simply.

2. **Self-assessment** – Tick the face that best describes your understanding of this concept.

3. **Question** – The question helps you to learn by doing. It is presented in a similar way to a National Test question and gives you a real example to work with.

4. **Flow chart** – This shows you the steps to use when completing questions like this. Some of the advice appears on every flow chart (e.g. 'Read the question then read it again'). This is because this is the best way of getting good marks in the test.

5. **Tip boxes** – These provide test hints and general tips on getting the best marks in the National Tests.

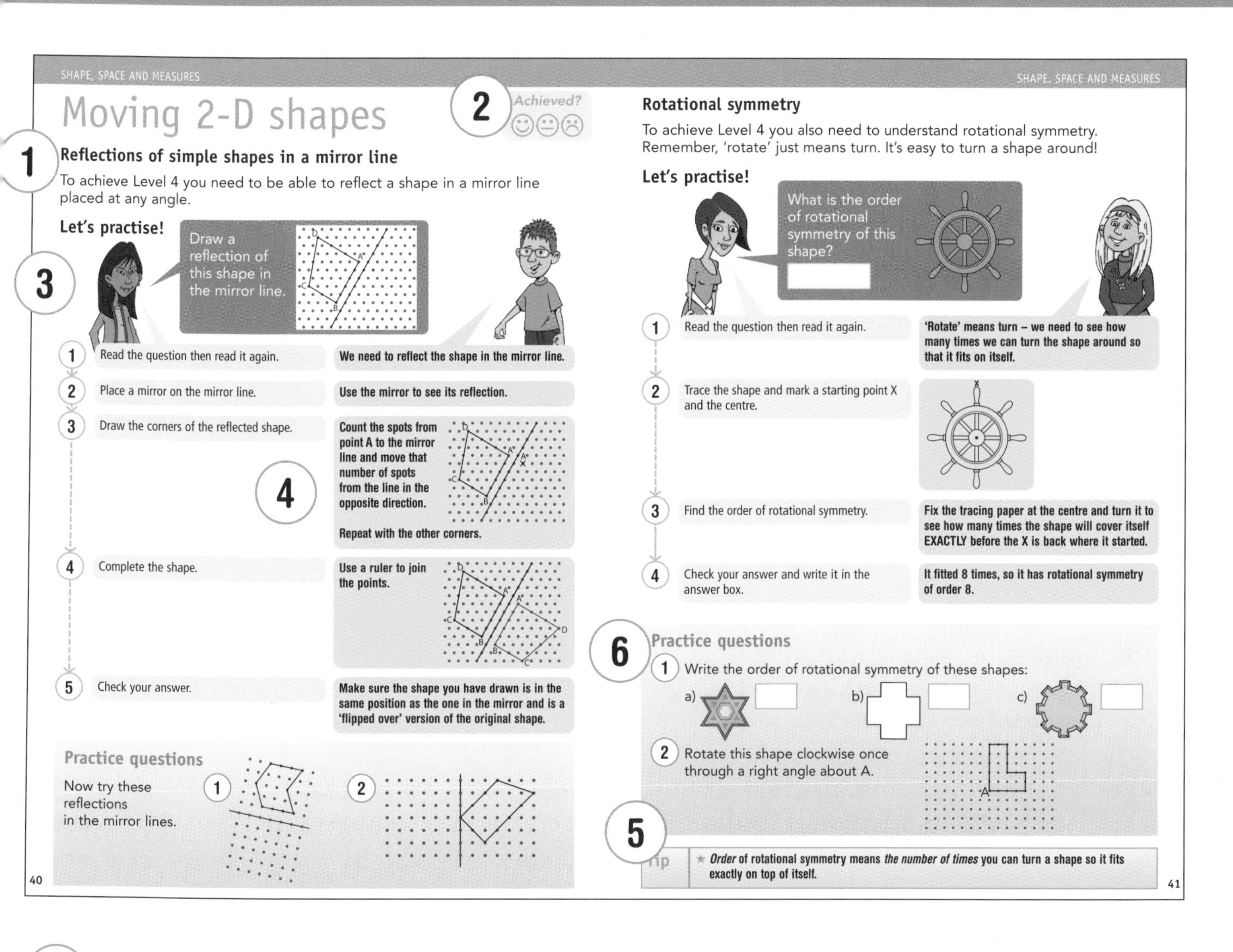

6 **Practice questions** – This is where you have to do the work! Try the question using the technique in the flow chart then check your answers at the back of the book. Practising questions is the best way to help improve your understanding.

GOOD LUCK!

Key facts*

NUMBER AND ALGEBRA

Counting and understanding number

Place value

- Each number is made up of digits. The position of the digit in a number gives it its value.

Hundreds	Tens	Units	tenths	hundredths	
7	8	4	3	5	
= 700 +	80 +	4 +	$\frac{3}{10}$ +	$\frac{5}{100}$ =	784.35

Estimating

- When rounding, remember 5 goes up! 6.785 rounds up to 6.79.

Positive and negative integers

- Integers are just whole numbers.
- When counting from negative up to positive or from positive down to negative, **remember to count 0!**
- When counting on a number line, count to the right when adding and to the left when subtracting.

Fractions

- A fraction is part of a whole number.

$\frac{1}{2}$

1 – the numerator: The numerator tells you how many equal parts are used.

2 – the denominator: The denominator tells you how many equal parts there are.

Reducing a fraction to its simplest form

- To reduce a fraction to its simplest form, find a common factor which you can divide into the numerator and the denominator. For example,

$$\frac{3 \div 3}{9 \div 3} = \frac{1}{3}$$

Fraction, decimal and percentage equivalents

- Remember as many of these as you can.

Fraction	$\frac{1}{2}$	$\frac{1}{10}$	$\frac{1}{4}$	$\frac{3}{4}$	Nearly $\frac{1}{3}$
Decimal	0.5	0.1	0.25	0.75	0.33
Percentage	50%	10%	25%	75%	33%

The vocabulary of ratio and proportion

- Ratio is 'to every'. For example, 2○ to every 3□ is ○○□□□
- Proportion is 'in every'. For example, 2○ in every 3 shapes could be shown as ○○□
- Reduce ratios and proportions to their simplest form. For example, 4:6 = 2:3.

Knowing and using number facts

- **Tables:** it is essential that you know these really well.
- **Squares:** numbers made when a number is multiplied by itself.
- **Multiples:** numbers that have been multiplied by a given number.
- **Factors:** numbers that can divide into a given number without leaving a remainder.

Checking your answers

- Inverse means opposite!
- Check addition by subtraction – and vice versa.
- Check division by multiplication – and vice versa.
- Use 'friendly numbers' when estimating: 2, 5, 10, etc.

Calculating

- Multiplying numbers by 10 and 100: push the digits to the left once for ×10 and twice for ×100.
- Dividing numbers by 10 and 100: push the digits to the right once for ÷10 and twice for ÷100.
- Addition and subtraction of decimals:
  1. Line up the decimal points when you write out the calculation.
  2. Fill empty places with a 0.
  3. Remember to put the decimal point in your answer!

Choosing your method

- Remember to look at the numbers you are working with. You might be able to use a good mental strategy rather than a written method.

* Important note for Teachers and Parents: These key facts relate to the Primary Mathematics Framework (2006) because pupils in Year 6 will continue to be taught and assessed against it in the academic year 2014–15.

SHAPE, SPACE AND MEASURES
Understanding shape

3-D shapes
- Vertices are corners.
- Faces are flat surfaces.
- Edges are edges!

2-D shapes
- Polygons have all straight sides.
- Regular polygons have sides all the same length.
- Parallel lines never meet – think of a train track!
- Perpendicular lines make a right angle.

Triangles
- An isosceles triangle has TWO EQUAL SIDES AND TWO EQUAL ANGLES. Picture an isosceles triangle as an arrow!
- A scalene triangle has THREE SIDES OF DIFFERENT LENGTHS and THREE ANGLES OF DIFFERENT SIZES. When picturing a scalene triangle, think of scaling a mountain that has an easy way up or a more difficult side to climb!
- A right-angled triangle can be isosceles or scalene.

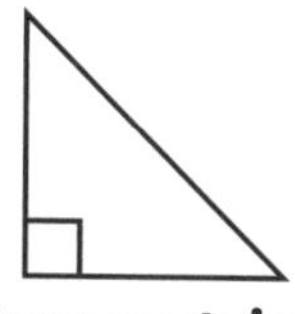
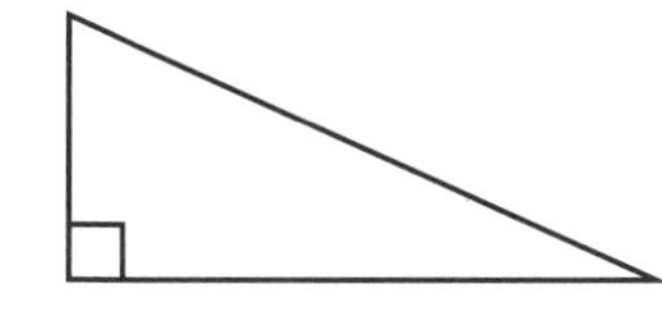

Symmetries
- When drawing reflections, remember to keep the correct distance from the mirror line.
- Remember, rotational symmetry is just working out how many ways the shape can fit EXACTLY on top of itself.

Angles
- Acute angle is between 0° and 89°
- Right angle = 90°
- Obtuse angle is between 91° and 179°
- Straight line = 180°
- Reflex angle is between 181° and 359°

Coordinates
- Always read ALONG the x axis and then UP/DOWN the y axis.
- Always write (x) before (y), i.e. (x, y).

Measuring

Measuring weight and capacity
- 1000 grams = 1 kilogram (1000 g = 1 kg)
- 1000 kilograms = 1 tonne (1000 kg = 1 tonne)
- 1000 millilitres = 1 litre (1000 ml = 1 l)

Estimating measures
- Milli = very small
- Centi = small
- Kilo = big

Perimeter
- Perimeter is the distance all the way round the edge of a flat shape.

Area
- Area is the space covered up by the shape.
- Count the squares and remember area is always measured in square units (cm^2, mm^2, m^2).

Reading scales
- CAREFULLY work out what each mark on the scale is worth.

HANDLING DATA

Pictograms
- With pictograms PICTURE = NUMBER

e.g. [ice cream] = 20 ice creams [half ice cream] = 10 ice creams

Mean, median, range and mode
- Mean = sum of all values divided by number of values
- Median = middle number in sequence (always write down in order first)
- Range = difference between highest and lowest number
- Mode = most common value

Charts and graphs
- Be careful and accurate. Use a sharp pencil.
- Pie charts are good for percentages, fractions or decimals.

USING AND APPLYING MATHEMATICS

Simple formulae
- Talk through the formula in your head. It will make it easier.

Number patterns
- Check the difference between the numbers to find the pattern.

About the National Tests

Key facts

- The Key Stage 2 National Tests take place in the summer term in Year 6. You will be tested on Maths and English.
- The tests take place in your school and will be marked by examiners – not your teacher!
- Individual test scores are not made public but a school's combined scores are published in what are commonly known as 'league tables'.

The 2015 Maths National Tests

The 2015 Maths tests will consist of three papers:

- **Mental Maths Test** – This test will be played to you on an audio CD. You will have to answer the questions mentally within 5, 10 or 15 seconds. This test will take about 20 minutes.
- **Paper 1** – This is a written mathematics paper, which will ask a range of mathematics questions on number, measurement, shape and data handling. Some questions will be worth 1 mark and others will be worth 2 marks. You will not be able to use a calculator but you should show any working out that you do as you may get a mark for a correct method, even if you get the wrong answer.
- **Paper 2** – This is the second written mathematics paper, which again will ask a range of mathematics questions on number, measurement, shape and data handling. Some questions will be worth 1 mark and others will be worth 2 marks as they will be more complex word problems. You will not be able to use a calculator but you should show any working out that you do as you may get a mark for a correct method, even if you get the wrong answer.

DON'T FORGET!

Using and applying mathematics
There are many questions testing how you use and apply your mathematical knowledge in different situations. This includes:

- knowing which is the important information in the questions
- how to check your results
- describing things mathematically using common symbols and diagrams
- explaining your reasons for conclusions that you make.

Much of the book is written to help you practice these questions. It is also worth looking at pages 53–60, which should help you with this area of maths.

You might be asked to explain your answers and also write possible answers. Remember, always show your method.

Test techniques

Before the test

1. When you revise, revise little and often rather than in long sessions. Use questions to check you really understand a topic.
2. Learn your multiplication facts up to 10 × 10 so that you can recall them instantly and quickly find related division facts.
3. Revise with a friend. You can encourage and learn from each other.
4. Get a good night's sleep the night before.
5. Be prepared – bring your own pens and pencils.

During the test

1. Don't rush the first few questions. These tend to be quite straightforward, so don't make any silly mistakes.
2. READ THE QUESTION THEN READ IT AGAIN.
3. If you get stuck, put a sensible guess and move on. You can come back to it later.
4. Never leave a multiple-choice question. Make an educated guess if you really can't work out the answer.
5. Check how many marks a question is worth. Has your answer 'earned' each mark?
6. Check each answer, perhaps using the inverse method or the rounding method. Does your answer look correct?
7. Be aware of the time. After 20 minutes, check to see how far you have got.
8. Try to leave a couple of minutes at the end to read through what you have written.
9. Always show your method as this may win a mark even if your answer is wrong.
10. Don't leave any questions unanswered. In the 2 minutes you have left yourself at the end, make an educated guess at the questions you really couldn't do.

Mental maths skills

To achieve Level 4 you need to develop your mental maths skills and know maths facts thoroughly.

Table facts

Know your tables to 10 × 10 really well.

You should know the division sums from your tables as well, so you can quickly answer questions like, 'How many 6s in 54?'

Number bonds

Quick recall of pairs of numbers that add to make multiples of 10 and 100 will be really useful in mental maths.

Place value

Make sure you are confident with place value up to 10 000 and decimals to 2 decimal places.

Fractions, decimals and percentages

Know the common values like tenths, quarters, halves and thirds. You might be asked for these.

Fraction	$\frac{1}{2}$	$\frac{1}{10}$	$\frac{1}{4}$	$\frac{3}{4}$	Nearly $\frac{1}{3}$
Decimal	0.5	0.1	0.25	0.75	0.33
Percentage	50%	10%	25%	75%	33%

Number properties

Know what factors, multiples and prime numbers are. You could be asked to identify or write these.

Simple formulae

You could be given fairly simple calculations where one of the numbers is replaced with a letter. Try making up and working out some calculations like this.

Number problems

Practise solving number problems in your head or by writing quick calculations. Lot of problems can involve money.

Angles

Practise identifying types of angles and make sure you know the shape and angle value of 1, 2, 3 and 4 right angles. Try to estimate angles of different sizes.

Shapes

Make sure you know about polygons and regular polygons for 2-D shapes. For 3-D shapes, names, faces, edges and vertices could be needed so make sure you know what the words mean!

Measures

Know the conversions of measure from small to big units like m to km and the other way round. Knowing the meanings of milli, centi and kilo really helps here.

Estimating measures

Learn the lengths, weights and capacities of some common objects. You can use these as a point of reference when you have to estimate other objects in the test.

Remember

You can write things down in mental maths, so you can write the calculations, but remember there is a time limit. The recording will carry on whether you have worked out the answer or not!

Fractions

Achieved?

To achieve Level 3 you need to use fractions and recognise when two fractions are equivalent.

A fraction is part of a 'whole number'.

A quarter or $\frac{1}{4}$ means 1 part out of 4 equal parts.
One quarter of this diagram has been shaded.

Three quarters or $\frac{3}{4}$ means 3 parts out of 4 equal parts.
Three quarters of this diagram have **not** been shaded.

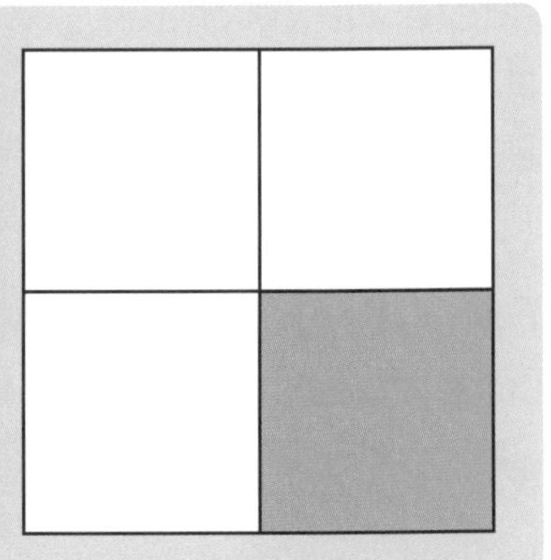

Have a look at the groups of marbles.

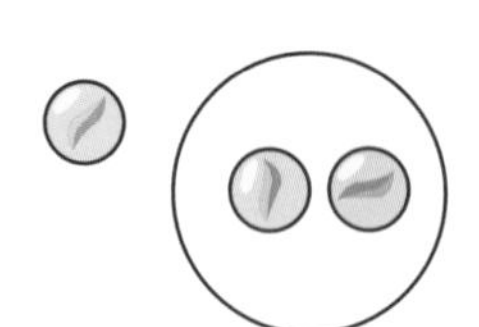

What fraction is circled? Answer $\frac{2}{3}$ or two thirds.

What fraction is not circled? Answer $\frac{1}{3}$ or one third.

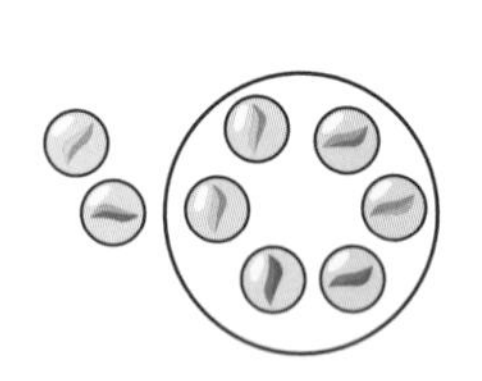

Try these questions.

What fraction is circled?

What fraction is not circled?

Equivalent fractions

Equivalent fractions are worth the same, even though they look different.

Eating $\frac{2}{4}$ of a cake is **the same as** or **equivalent to** eating $\frac{1}{2}$ a cake.

Look at this chart of equivalent fractions.

Look at one half ($\frac{1}{2}$). Can you see it is equivalent to (the same as): $\frac{2}{4}$, $\frac{3}{6}$ and $\frac{4}{8}$?

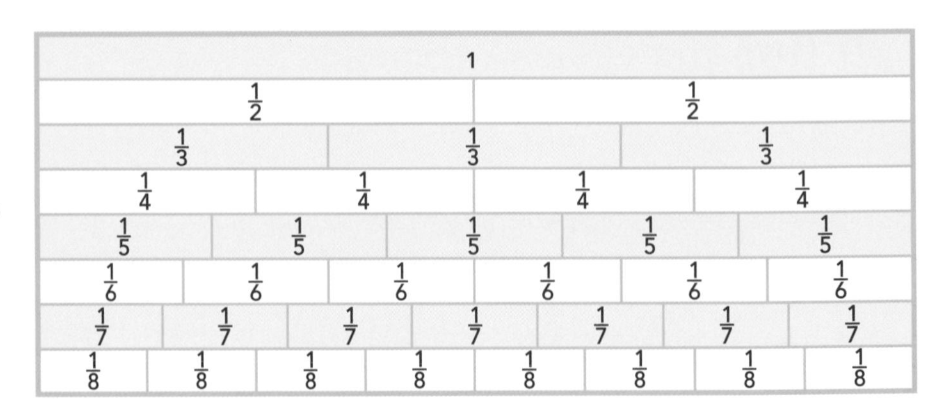

Study the chart to find more equivalent fractions. Write two here:

☐ is the same as ☐ ☐ is the same as ☐

Classifying shapes

Achieved?

3-D (three-dimensional) shapes

To achieve Level 4, you need to be able to describe 3-D shapes using the correct words.

3-D shapes are solid shapes. They are made up of faces, edges and vertices.

- A face is a flat surface of a solid shape.
- An edge is where two faces meet.
- A vertex is a corner.

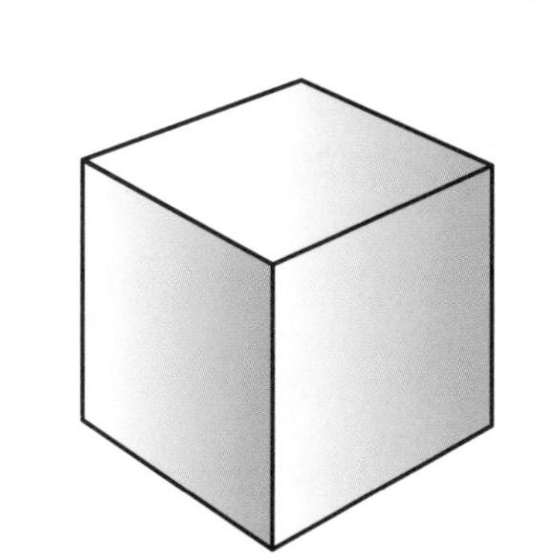

When looking at pictures of 3-D shapes you have to imagine the bits you can't see.

This picture of a cube shows 3 faces but, of course, there are actually 6!

Complete this chart. Try to picture the shapes in your mind.

	Cone	Cylinder	Sphere	Cuboid	Triangular-based pyramid	Triangular prism
Number of faces						
Number of edges						
Number of vertices						

2-D (two-dimensional) shapes

2-D shapes are 'flat shapes'. If they have straight sides they are called polygons. If they have straight sides and all the angles and sides are equal they are called regular polygons.

Symmetry

A shape is symmetrical (has symmetry) if you can draw a mirror line so that each side matches. This is also called 'reflective symmetry'. Take a look:

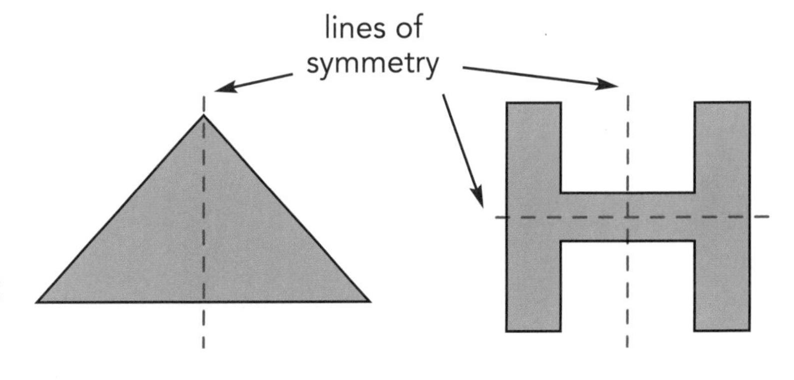

Bar charts and pictograms

This step-by-step approach gives you a system so that you can read charts and graphs accurately. That's important if you want to achieve Level 4!

1. Read the information carefully. — **What is the graph or chart trying to tell you?**
2. On a graph, check what each axis represents. — **Check the numbers going up the side (the *y* axis). Do they go up in 1s, 2s, 5s or 10s?**
3. On a pictogram, check what each symbol (picture) represents. — **If one symbol is worth two sandwiches, for example, what is half the symbol worth?**
4. Read the question then read it again. Find the row or column with the information you need and work out the amounts using the numbers or symbols. — **Use your finger or ruler to help you. ALWAYS double-check your answer.**

Practice questions

Here is a bar chart showing the favourite sandwich fillings in Year 6.

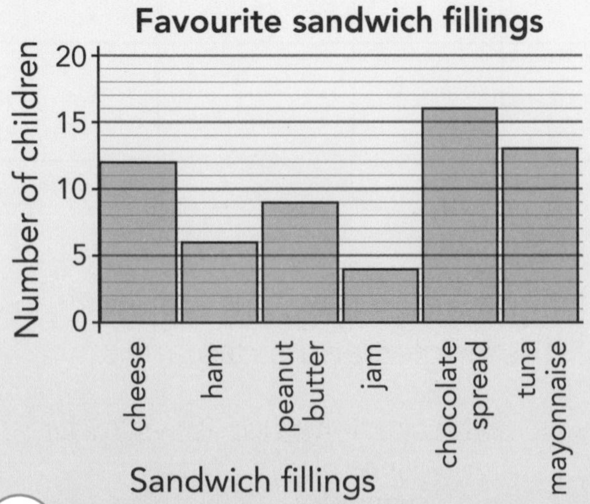

Here is the same information in a pictogram. A pictogram uses symbols to show a group of units.

cheese

ham

peanut butter

jam

chocolate spread

tuna mayonnaise

= 2 children

= 1 child

1. Which is the second most popular filling?
2. How many more children like chocolate spread than peanut butter?
3. How many children in total like cheese or ham fillings?

Decimal notation and negative numbers

Money

We use 'decimal notation' to record money and show pounds and pence. A penny is one hundredth of a pound.

Five pounds forty-two is written like this:

Before the decimal point is the number of whole pounds.

After the decimal point is the fraction of a pound (or number of pence).

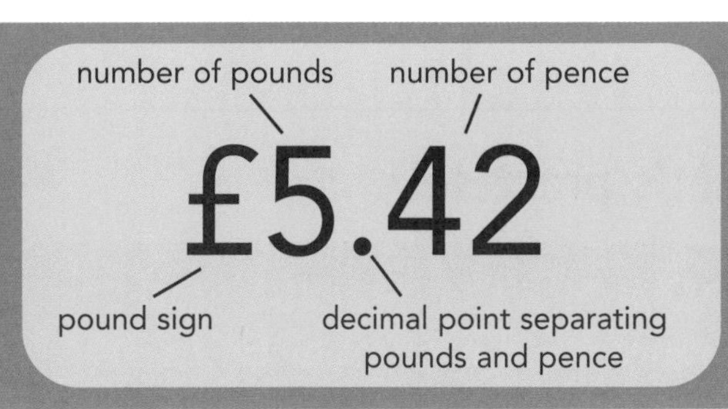

For each of these amounts, write the number of pounds and number of pence:

Tip

★ **When writing money ALWAYS put two digits after the decimal point.**
For example: £3 and 5p = £3.05 (not £3.5 or £3.50)
£7 and 40p = £7.40 (not £7.4 or £7.04)

Temperature

Negative numbers are numbers below zero. Thermometers measure temperature and use numbers below zero (0°C) when it is freezing.

a)

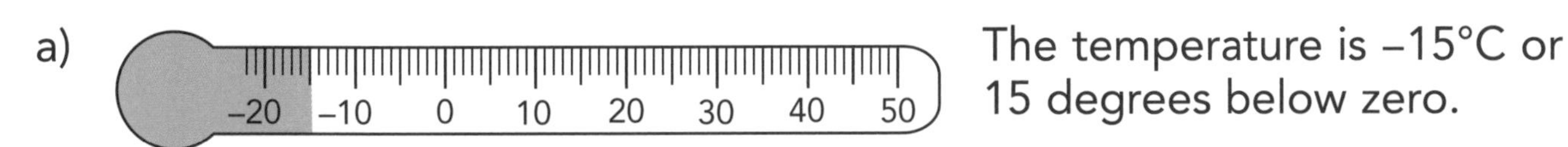

The temperature is –15°C or 15 degrees below zero.

b)

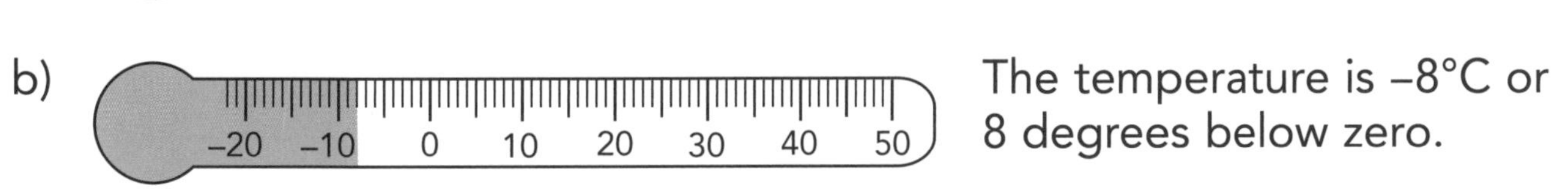

The temperature is –8°C or 8 degrees below zero.

Which do you think is colder? a) or b)?

Tip

★ **Think of a thermometer like a number line and don't forget to include zero when counting up and down the scale.**
The greater the negative number on a thermometer, the colder it is.

Place value

To achieve Level 4 you need to understand that decimals are numbers that come in between whole numbers. Look at 3.8 on the number line. We say '3 point 8'. It has one decimal place (8 tenths). To achieve Level 4 you need to use and understand decimals with up to three decimal places: tenths, hundredths and thousandths.

0 1 2 3 3.8 4 5 6

Let's practise!

What are the digits 3 and 6 worth in the number 54.673?

1	Read the question then read it again.	**We need to know the value of 3 and 6.**
2	Write the number.	**54.673 is in between 54 and 55.**
3	Work out what the digits stand for.	**Use** H T U . tenths hundredths thousandths — 5 4 . 6 7 3 — **So 3 means $\frac{3}{1000}$ and 6 means $\frac{6}{10}$**
4	Does your answer look sensible? If not, go back to step 3.	**Yes, the columns are labelled correctly.**

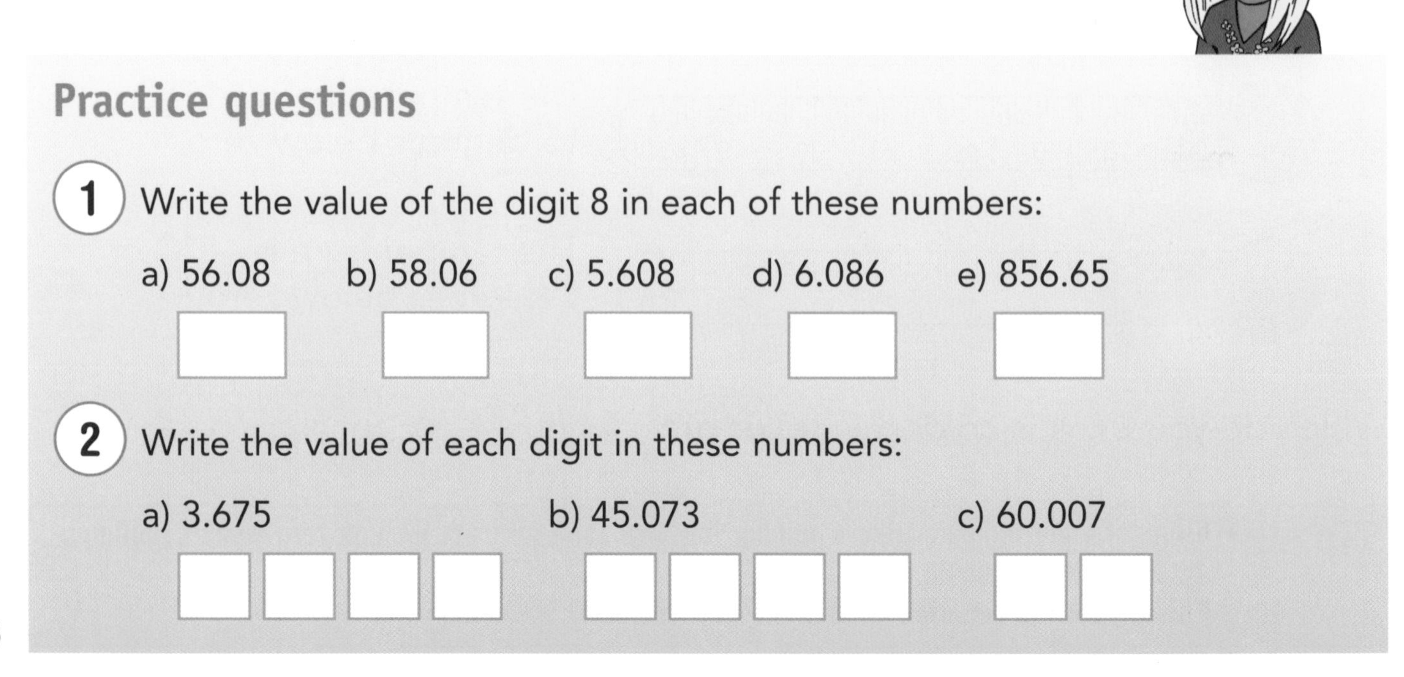

Practice questions

1. Write the value of the digit 8 in each of these numbers:

   a) 56.08 b) 58.06 c) 5.608 d) 6.086 e) 856.65

2. Write the value of each digit in these numbers:

   a) 3.675 b) 45.073 c) 60.007

To achieve Level 4 you must show you can order decimal numbers.

Let's practise!

These are the distances jumped in the long jump competition at the school sports day by class 6C.

Keeley 3.65 m	Jamie 3.75 m	Dominic 2.73 m
Ellie 3.3 m	Harry 2.79 m	Seniz 2.7 m

Write down the distances in order of size, starting with the furthest jump.

1st ____ 2nd ____ 3rd ____

4th ____ 5th ____ 6th ____

1. Read the question then read it again. — **Lots to read here. Be careful! 'Furthest' means 'highest number'.**

2. List the numbers, lining up the decimal points. — **3.65 Remember to put zeros in any spaces.**
3.75
2.73
3.30
2.79
2.70

3. Order the numbers. Find the highest, then the next highest. Write them down. — **3.75 is highest, then 3.65.**

4. Continue until all the numbers are ordered. — **Now 3.30, followed by 2.79. 2.73 is further than 2.70.**

5. Check the order is sensible. If not, go back to step 2. — **3.75, 3.65, 3.3, 2.79, 2.73, 2.7 These are in size order.**

Practice questions

Put these decimals in order. Start with the **smallest** number.

1. 5.68, 5.86, 58.6, 56.8, 5.66

2. 8.456, 8.546, 8.654, 8.564, 8.645

3. 4.7, 7.5, 7.4, 7.3, 7.9, 4.9

4. 3.66 km, 36.6 km, 36.36 km, 3.36 km, 3.663 km

Multiplying by 10 and 100

Achieved? ☺ 😐 ☹

At Level 4 you have to multiply whole numbers by 10 and 100.

Multiplication

To multiply a whole number by 10, push the digits one place to the left and put in a zero to fill the units space, e.g. $68 \times 10 = 680$.

To multiply a whole number by 100, push the digits two places to the left and put in two zeros to fill the tens and units spaces, e.g. $68 \times 100 = 6800$.

Let's practise!

Write in the answer.

$346 \times 10 =$ ☐

1	Read the question then read it again.	**346 x 10 = ?**
2	Remember the rules!	**To multiply a number by 10, we push the digits one place to the left and put in a zero.**
3	Calculate.	**H T U 3 4 6 × 10 becomes Th H T U 3 4 6 0**
4	Check your answer. If it doesn't look correct, go back to step 2.	**Does 3460 look sensible? We've multiplied by 10 so we only put in one zero. Our answer looks correct.**

Tip ★ **To multiply 30 by 40, use $3 \times 4 = 12$ and then push the digits two places to the left because there are 2 zeros, so $30 \times 40 = 1200$.**

Practice questions

1. $76 \times 10 =$ ☐
2. $580 \times$ ☐ $= 58{,}000$
3. $543 \times 100 =$ ☐
4. $40 \times 20 =$ ☐
5. $60 \times 300 =$ ☐
6. ☐ $\times 10 = 650$

Dividing by 10 and 100

Achieved? ☺ 😐 ☹

At Level 4 you have to divide whole numbers by 10 and 100.

To divide a whole number by 10, push the digits one place to the right, so you lose a zero, e.g. 680 ÷ 10 = 68.

To divide a whole number by 100, push the digits two places to the right, losing two zeros, e.g. 6800 ÷ 100 = 68.

Let's practise!

Write in the missing number.

6500 ÷ ☐ = 65

1	Read the question then read it again.	**6500 ÷ ☐ = 65**
2	Remember the rules!	**How many places to the right have the digits been pushed?**
3	Calculate.	**Push the digits once: 6500 → 650** **We need to get 65, so push the digits again.** **650 → 65** **The digits moved 2 places so the answer is 100.**
4	Check the answer. If it looks sensible, write it in the box. If not, go back to step 2.	**6500 ÷ 100 = 65 looks fine. Multiplying is the opposite of dividing so we can check by doing 65 × 100 = 6500. We are correct!**

Tip ★ **For 640 ÷ 80 we can push the digits to the right, losing a zero, to make 64 ÷ 8 = 8.**

Practice questions

1. 8400 ÷ 10 = ☐
2. 2500 ÷ ☐ = 250
3. 5000 ÷ 100 = ☐
4. 75,000 ÷ ☐ = 750
5. 4500 ÷ 50 = ☐
6. 42,000 ÷ 600 = ☐

Addition

To achieve Level 4, you need to be able to add several numbers, including some greater than 1000.

Let's practise!

What is the total of 682, 52 and 2827?

1. Read the question then read it again.

   'Total of' means it's an addition.

2. Write the numbers. Estimate an answer.

   Round and estimate: 700 + 50 + 2800 = 3550

3. Write the digits in the correct columns.

Th	H	T	U
	6	8	2
		5	2
+2	8	2	7

4. Start by adding the units.

Th	H	T	U
	6	8	2
		5	2
+2	8	2	7
			1
		1	

   If the total is over 9, carry the tens digit to the next column.

5. Now work across the sum with the tens, then the hundreds, and then the thousands.

Th	H	T	U
	6	8	2
		5	2
+2	8	2	7
3	5	6	1
1	1	1	

   Again, for any total over 9 carry the tens digit to the next column.

6. Check your answer against your estimate. Does it look right? If not, go back to step 2.

   3561 is very close to 3550.

Practice questions

1. Find the total of 648, 93 and 8752.
2. Increase 8654 by 7985.
3. What is 675 more than 8675 plus 938?
4. Add together 745, 8, 7385 and 68.

Subtraction

Achieved?

To achieve Level 4, you need to be able to subtract numbers, including some greater than 1000.

Let's practise!

Find the difference between 4734 and 497.

1. Read the question then read it again.
   'Find the difference between'… it's a subtraction.

2. Picture the numbers. Estimate an answer.
   Round the numbers and estimate: 4700 – 500 = 4200

3. Line up the digits in the correct columns.

Th	H	T	U
4	7	3	4
–	4	9	7

4. Start with the right hand (units) column and subtract the bottom number from the top. If the bottom number is bigger then 'exchange' a ten from the tens.

Th	H	T	U
4	7	~~3~~ 2	1 4
–	4	9	7
		3	7

5. Repeat with the tens column, remembering to exchange if the bottom number is bigger than the top number. Repeat with the hundreds and then the thousands.

Th	H	T	U
4	~~7~~ 6	~~3~~ 12	1 4
–	4	9	7
4	2	3	7

6. Check your answer against your estimate. Does it look right? If not, go back to step 2.
   Our estimate was 4200. Pretty close to the right answer! That's great.

Practice questions

1. Subtract 6754 from 8572. ☐
2. Find the difference between 578 and 6350. ☐
3. What is 6492 minus 879? ☐
4. Decrease 7563 by 777. ☐

Short multiplication

Achieved?

At Level 4 short multiplication is two- or three-digit numbers multiplied by a single-digit number. You can use grids like the one in the flow chart for these calculations.

Let's practise!

What is the product of 482 and 9?

1. Read the question then read it again. — **'Product of' … that's multiplication!**
2. Picture the numbers. Estimate an answer. — **Mmm …
500 × 10 …
Around 5000?**
3. Partition the numbers and draw a grid.

×	400	80	2
9			

4. Multiply the numbers.

×	400	80	2
9	*3600*	*720*	*18*

5. Add up the answers. — **3600 + 720 + 18 = 4338**
6. Check your answers. Does it look right? If not, go back to step 2. — **What did I estimate the answer was? About 5000.**
7. Check your answer against your estimate. Does it look right? If not, go back to step 2. — **Our answer was fairly close to the estimate. Yes! We were correct.**

Practice questions

1. 486 × 4 = ☐
2. 635 × 8 = ☐
3. Times 694 by 5. ☐
4. Multiply 805 by 7. ☐
5. What is the product of 742 and 6? ☐
6. What is 379 multiplied by 9? ☐

Short division

Achieved? ☺ 😐 ☹

At Level 4 short division is two- or three-digit numbers divided by a single-digit number. Remember, division is the inverse (or opposite) of multiplication.

Let's practise!

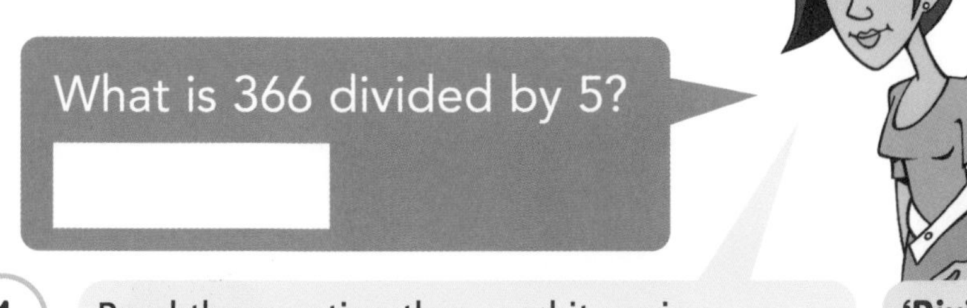

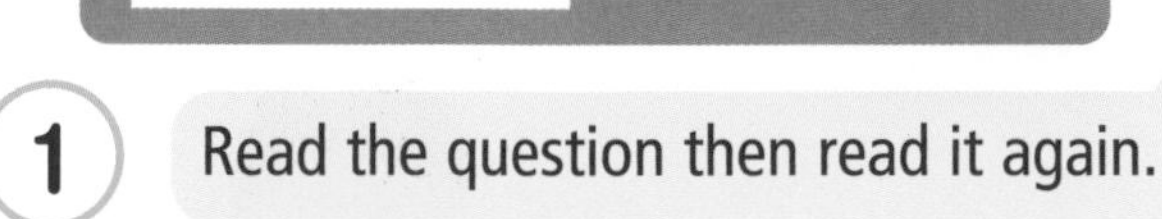

1. Read the question then read it again. — **'Divided by' … that's division.**

2. Write the numbers. What is the task? — **How many times does 5 fit into 366?**

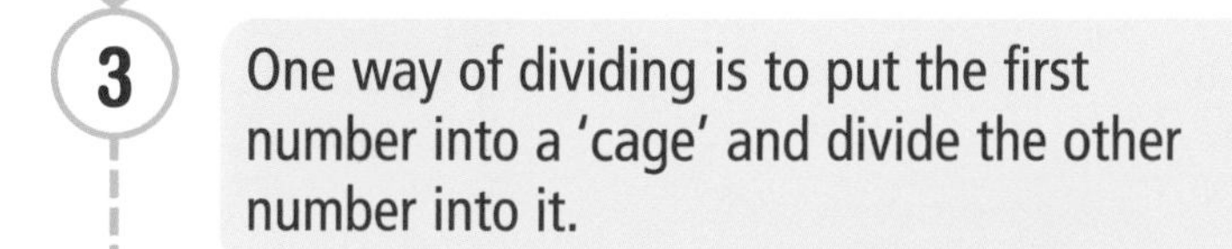

3. One way of dividing is to put the first number into a 'cage' and divide the other number into it. — **366 ÷ 5.366 is the first number.**

   $5\overline{)3\ 6\ 6}$

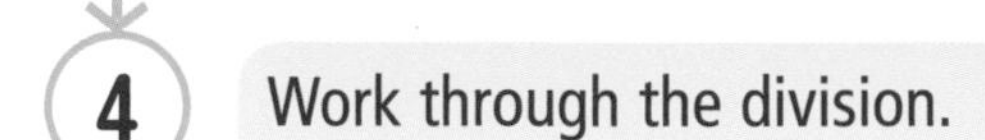

4. Work through the division. — **Think about the hundreds. There are 3 hundreds. You are trying to make groups of 5. If you only have 3 you can't make any groups of 5 so put the hundreds in with the tens to make 36 tens.**

   $5\overline{)3\ {}^{3}6\ 6}$

   So how many 5s make 36? That's 7 and 1 ten left over. Put the left-over ten with the units.

   $\begin{array}{r} 7\ \ \\ 5\overline{)3\ {}^{3}6\ {}^{1}6} \end{array}$

   Next, how many 5s in 16? That's 3 and 1 left over.

   $\begin{array}{r} 7\ 3\ \text{r1} \\ 5\overline{)3\ {}^{3}6\ {}^{1}6} \end{array}$

   Our answer is 73 r1.

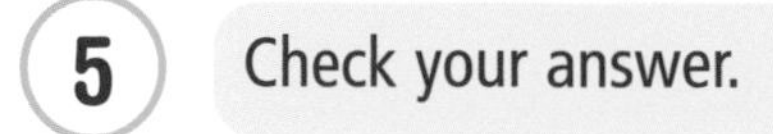

5. Check your answer. — **73 rounds to 70 and 5 × 70 = 350**
   Our answer is sensible!

Practice questions

1. 677 ÷ 2 = ☐
2. 532 ÷ 3 = ☐
3. 614 ÷ 4 = ☐
4. 953 ÷ 6 = ☐

Adding and subtracting decimals

Achieving Level 4 means knowing how to add and subtract decimals. When we add or subtract decimals we must line up the decimal points.

Let's practise!

5.76 kg + 18.6 kg = ☐

1. Read the question then read it again.
2. Write the numbers. Estimate an answer.
   5.76 is nearly 6 and 18.6 is nearly 19. 6 kg + 19 kg = 25 kg
3. Write the numbers, lining up the decimal points.
   ```
      5.76
   + 18.6
   ```
4. Fill in any spaces in the columns with 0 then calculate the sum.
   ```
     05.76
   + 18.60
     24.36
     1 1
   ```
5. Does it look right? If not, go back to step 3 and check you have lined up the decimal points.
   24.36 kg is close to 25 kg.

Practice questions

Use the flow chart to work out these additions.

1. 7.84 + 6.97 ☐
2. 64.7 m + 58.8 m ☐
3. £2.87 + £16.65 ☐

Find the difference between these numbers.

4. 53.75 and 24.58 ☐
5. 6.75 and 12.8 ☐
6. 56.34 g and 28.69 g ☐

Ratio and proportion

Achieved? ☺ 😐 ☹

To achieve Level 4 you need to know how to read and to understand the vocabulary of ratio and proportion.

Ratio

Ratio compares one part of a set to another part.

Let's practise!

What is the ratio of purple flowers to orange flowers?

1	Read the question then read it again.	**We are comparing purple and orange flowers.**
2	Write the numbers.	**There are 7 purple and 5 orange flowers.**
3	Write the ratio.	**There are 7 purple flowers to 5 orange flowers. (This can be written 7:5.)**
4	Check your answer.	**We have counted correctly.**

Proportion

Proportion compares one part of a set to the whole set.

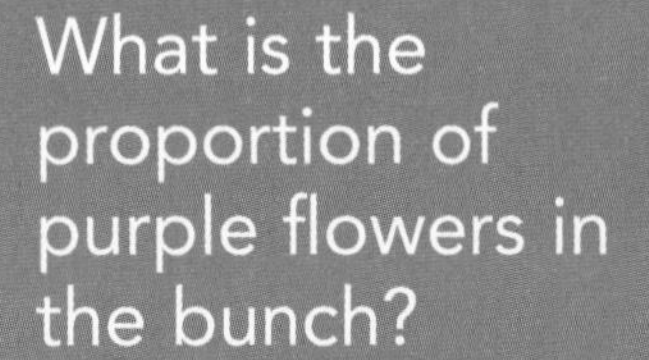

What is the proportion of purple flowers in the bunch?

Let's practise!

1	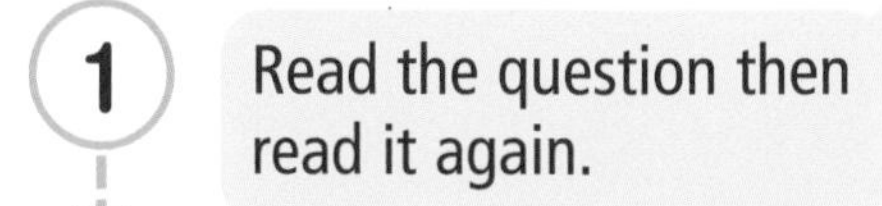 Read the question then read it again.	 **We are comparing purple flowers to the whole bunch of flowers.**
2	Write the numbers.	**There are 7 purple flowers and 12 flowers.**
3	Write the proportion.	**There are 7 purple flowers out of the 12 flowers. (This can be written $\frac{7}{12}$.)**
4	Check your answer.	**We have counted correctly.**

Practice questions

1. What is the ratio of red sweets to green sweets? ☐
2. What is the proportion of green sweets? ☐

Checking your answers

Checking your results should be something you do automatically when you answer a question. It can save you marks in a test and help you to become more accurate with your answers.

Here are some excellent ways you can check the results of your calculations.

Inverse operations

Remember, adding and subtracting are OPPOSITES. Multiplying and dividing are OPPOSITES. We can use this knowledge to check our answers quickly.

Examples:
170 – 95 = 75 Check: 75 + 95 = 170
228 ÷ 6 = 38 Check: 38 × 6 = 228

Practice questions

1. 524 – 67 = ☐ Check: ☐ + 67 = ☐
2. 160 ÷ 4 = ☐ Check: ☐ × 4 = ☐
3. 7884 – 897 = ☐ Check: ☐ + 897 = ☐
4. 2250 ÷ 50 = ☐ Check: ☐ × 50 = ☐

Approximate by rounding

Another way to check your answers is to round the numbers in the question up or down to the nearest 10, 100 or 1000. This will give you a simple sum to do first and give you a rough answer.

Example:
297 + 805 is about 300 + 800 Easy! 1100
38 × 19 is about 40 × 20 Easy! 800

You can then check your final answer against your rough answer – they should be fairly close. If not, check your rough answer and then your calculation.

Practice questions

Final answer

5. 687 × 11 = Rough answer ____________________ ☐

6. 391 – 108 = Rough answer ____________________ ☐

7. 468 ÷ 18 = Rough answer ____________________ ☐

Forwards and backwards

When adding several numbers together, try adding them again but backwards. It doesn't matter what order you add numbers together, the answer will be the same.

Example:
11 + 12 + 13 = 36 or 13 + 12 + 11 = 36

Try this sum, starting from the top of the units column. Now check by starting at the bottom of the units column and continuing. Were you correct?

$$\begin{array}{r} 374 \\ 536 \\ 28 \\ +\quad 73 \\ \hline \\ \hline \end{array}$$

Addition

- If you add two even numbers, your answer is even.
- If you add two odd numbers, your answer is even.
- If you add one odd and one even number, your answer is odd.

Subtraction

- If you find the difference of two even numbers, your answer is even.
- If you find the difference of two odd numbers, your answer is even.
- If you find the difference of one odd and one even number, your answer is odd.

Multiplication

- If you multiply two even numbers, your answer is even.
- If you multiply two odd numbers, your answer is odd.
- If you multiply one odd and one even number, your answer is even.

Practice questions

Let's test if the rules we've learnt are always true.

1. 9228 + 132 = ☐
2. 157 + 1211 = ☐
3. 3409 + 2652 = ☐
4. 9876 – 5642 = ☐
5. 4009 – 1031 = ☐
6. 7797 – 3219 = ☐
7. 564 × 6 = ☐
8. 139 × 3 = ☐
9. 246 × 7 = ☐

Proportions of a whole

Achieved?

To achieve Level 4 you need to be able to find a simple proportion (part) of a whole as a decimal, a fraction or a percentage.

Percentages

'Per cent' means 'out of 100'.

Let's practise!

What percentage of this shape is shaded?

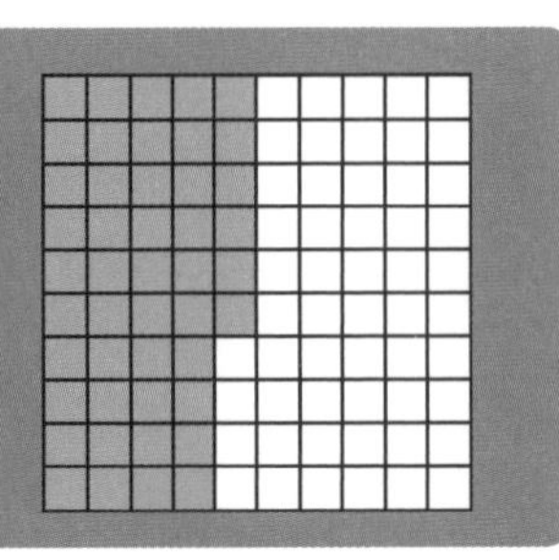

1	Read the question then read it again.	**We need to find the percentage.**
2	Count the squares in the grid.	**There are 10 rows of 10 squares, which make 100 squares.**
3	Count the number of coloured squares.	**4 columns of 10 are coloured, and 6 are coloured in another column. This makes 46 squares.**
4	Express the shaded amounted as part of 100.	**There are 46 out of 100 coloured.**
5	Express this as a percentage.	**46 'out of 100' is the same as 46 per cent, so 46% is shaded.**
6	Check your answer.	**46% is just less than $\frac{1}{2}$, and we can see that slightly less than $\frac{1}{2}$ the shape is coloured.**

Practice questions

1. What percentage of these squares is shaded?

a) 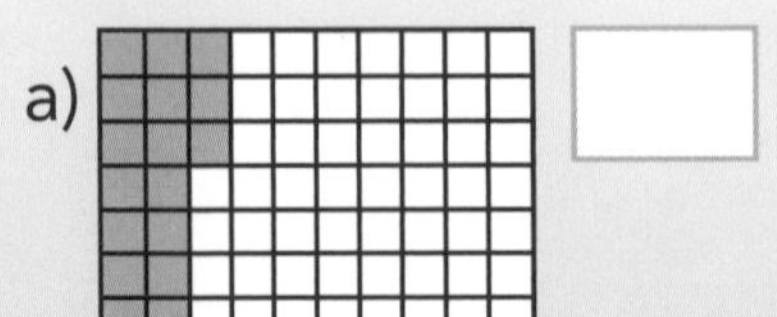

b)

c) 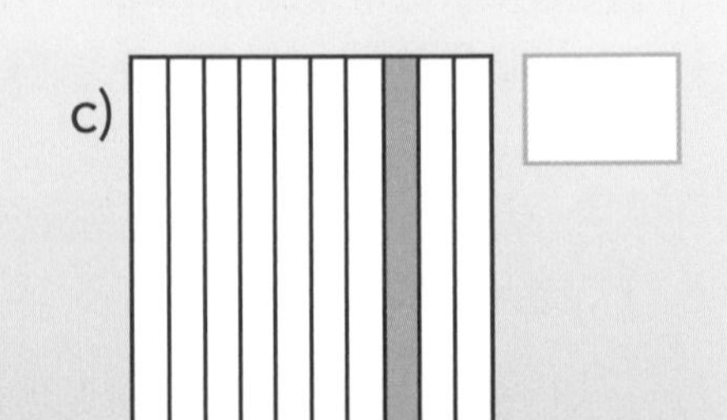

2. Write the percentage of each of the above squares that is **not** shaded.

a)

b)

c)

Important proportions

Achieved? ☺ 😐 ☹

Important proportions of whole objects

Parts of whole objects can be written in different ways. To achieve Level 4 you need to learn these proportions:

Halves ($\frac{1}{2}$) or 50% or 0.5

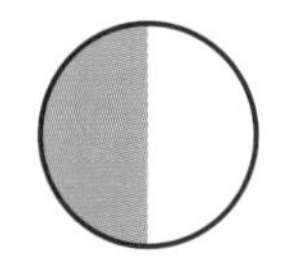

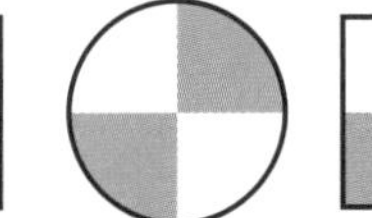
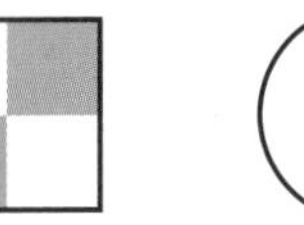

Quarters ($\frac{1}{4}$) or 25% or 0.25

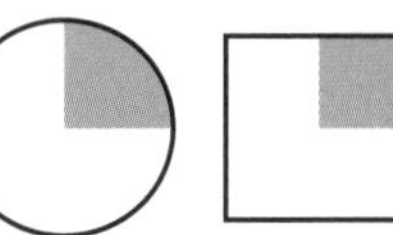
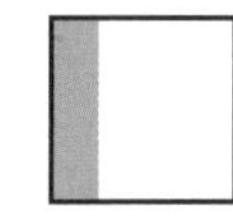
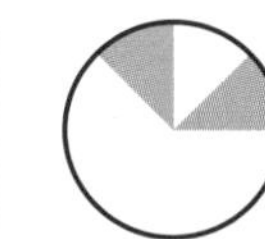
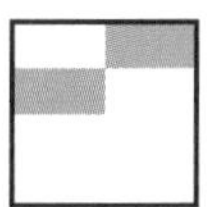

Three quarters ($\frac{3}{4}$) or 75% or 0.75

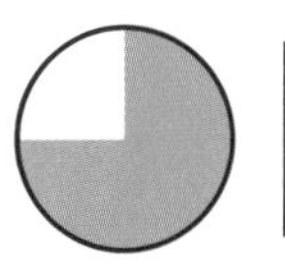
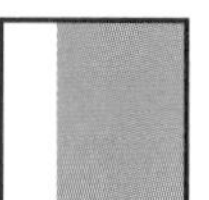

Tenths ($\frac{1}{10}$) or 10% or 0.1

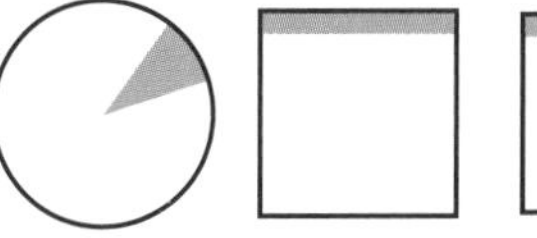
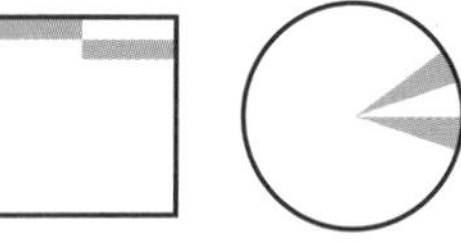

Thirds ($\frac{1}{3}$) or 33% (approx.) or 0.33 (approx.)

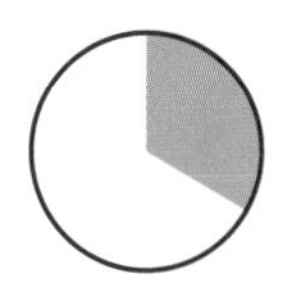

Two thirds or ($\frac{2}{3}$) or 66% (approx.) or 0.66 (approx.)

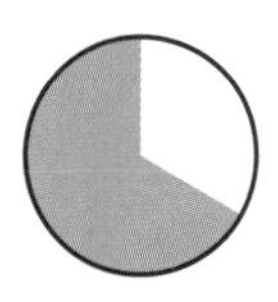

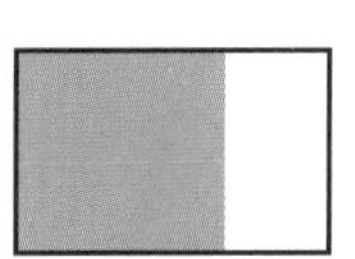

Practice question

Try this question. You need to use what you have learnt about proportions to help you find the answers.

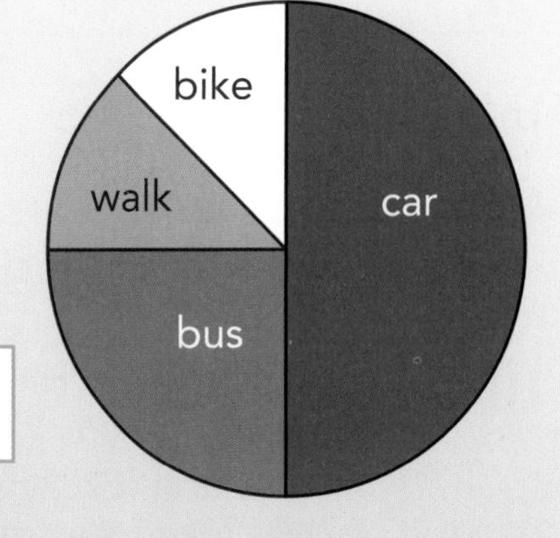

160 people went past school in an hour. Class A wrote down how they were travelling.

a) Which transport was chosen by 80 people? (Can you see the part that shows 80 out of 160? This is half of the total.)

b) How many people were travelling on the bus? (Can you see the shape of the number of people travelling by bus? It is a quarter.)

Number relationships

Achieved?

To achieve Level 4 you need to understand and identify factors, square numbers and multiples.

Factors

Factors are numbers that divide exactly into other numbers.

The factors of 12 are: 1, 2, 3, 4, 6 and 12.

The factors of 10 are: 1, 2, 5 and 10.

Practice questions

List all the factors of:

1. 24
2. 35
3. 49
4. 64

Square numbers

Square numbers are made when you multiply a number by itself.

Example: 4 squared is $4 \times 4 = 16$

They are called square numbers because the multiplication rows make a square. Can you find all the square numbers up to 100?

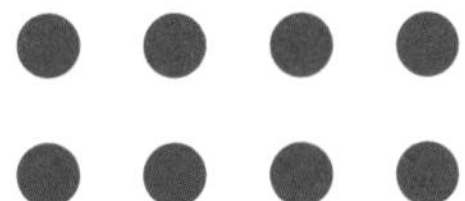

Tip

★ **You need to know all the times tables up to 10 for Level 4. Knowing the square numbers helps.**

Multiples

Multiples are made by multiplying one number by another. Think of multiple as **'made by multiplying by'**. So multiples of 5 are made by multiplying by 5.

Tips

- ★ **If a number is a multiple of 2, the last digit will be even. (20, 22, 24, 26)**
- ★ **If a number is a multiple of 3, the sum of its digits can be divided by 3. (57 = 5 + 7 = 12 or 114 = 1 + 1 + 4 = 6)**
- ★ **If a number is a multiple of 4, the last two digits can be divided by 4. (780 or 436 or 916)**
- ★ **If a number is a multiple of 5, the last digit is a 0 or a 5. (1055, 260, 475)**
- ★ **If a number is a multiple of 6, it must be an even number and the sum of its digits must be divisible by 3. (1488 = 1 + 4 + 8 + 8 = 21)**
- ★ **If a number is a multiple of 7, it is a tricky one and you will just have to work it out the long way. 7 is awkward, it doesn't like rules!**
- ★ **If a number is a multiple of 8, then half the number can be divided by 4. (528 ÷ 2 = 264 ÷ 4 = 66)**
- ★ **If a number is a multiple of 9, then the sum of its digits is divisible by 9. (378 = 3 + 7 + 8 = 18)**
- ★ **If a number is a multiple of 10, then the last digit is 0. (290, 1000, 2020)**

Using simple formulae

Achieved?

A formula is a way of explaining a rule. To achieve Level 4 you need to be able to explain a given rule in writing.

Let's practise!

Explain how to find the number of months in any number of years.

1	Read the question then read it again.	**It is all words. You have to work out any numbers involved.**
2	Picture the numbers and the words.	**The key word here is 'explain'. You also need to say that there are 12 months in a year.**
3	Talk through the rule in your head.	**To find the number of months in any number of years, you must multiply the number of years by 12 …**
4	Test your rule. Does it work? If not, go back to step 1.	**Make your test simple to avoid mistakes, e.g. 4 years = 4 × 12 = 48 months**
5	Write your rule as simply as possible.	**'The number of months in any number of years = the number of years multiplied by 12.'**
6	Check your answer. Does it make sense?	**Read it through to yourself. Does your formula work?**

Tips

- **Rehearse your sentences in your head before you write them. When you have written them, read them back to yourself. Have you thought clearly? Have you said what you wanted to say?**
- **The '=' sign means 'the same as'**
  e.g. 2 + 2 = 4 — 2 + 2 is the same as 4
  10 – 5 = 8 – 3 — 10 – 5 is the same as 8 – 3

Using coordinates

Achieved? ☺ 😐 ☹

To achieve Level 4 you need to be able to read and plot coordinates of points on grids, like maps and charts.

On a grid the numbers going **across** are on the **x** axis.
The numbers going **up** and **down** are on the **y** axis.
The **x** number (across) always comes first!

Let's practise!

Look at this map of a theme park. What are the coordinates of the pirate ship?

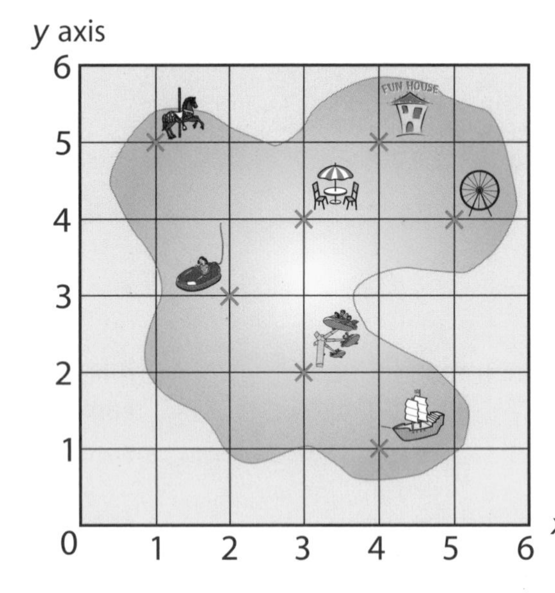

1	Read the question then read it again.	**We are being asked to find a coordinate pair.**
2	Find the place named.	**The pirate ship is at the point 4 across and 1 up. The coordinates are (4, 1).**
3	Write the numbers.	**We need to use the numbers on the map.**
4	Check your answer.	**If we find (4, 1) on the map, that is where the pirate ship is. We are correct!**

Practice questions

Use the map to answer these questions.

1. What are the coordinates of:

   a) the flying cars? ☐ b) the café? ☐ c) the carousel? ☐

2. Which ride is at these points?

   a) (2, 3) ____________________ b) (4, 5) ____________________

Coordinate problems often use shapes

Let's practise!

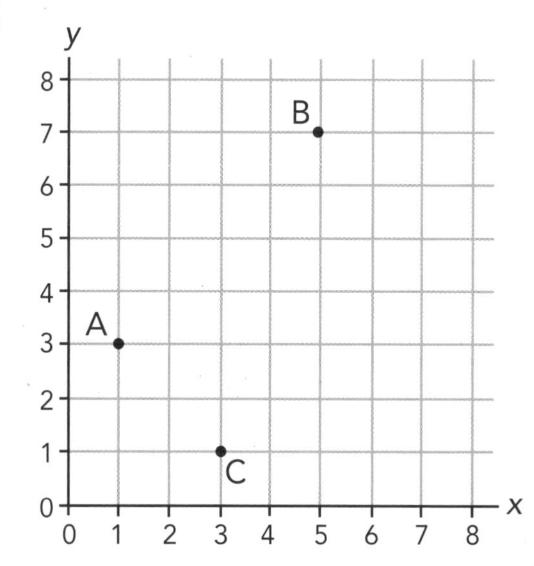

Look at the points that are marked. Mark a fourth point to make a rectangle. What are its coordinates?

1. Read the question then read it again. — **We have to make a rectangle.**
2. Study the points given. — **There are three points.**
3. Look for clues from the shape and the points. — **A rectangle has right angles. Joining A to B and then A to C makes a right angle.**

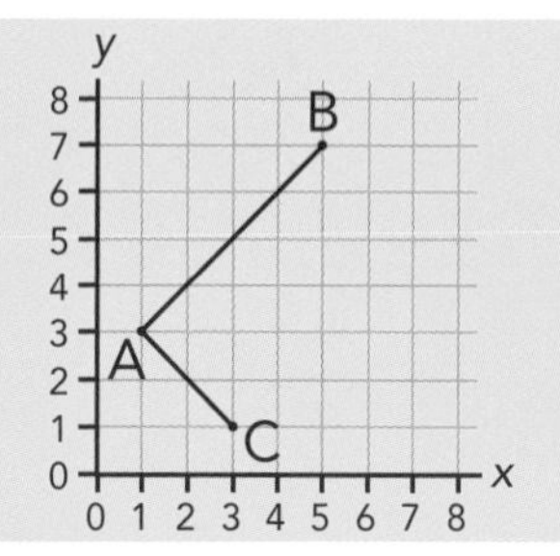

4. Complete the shape. — **Make right angles at points B and C and draw the lines. Look for where the lines cross.**

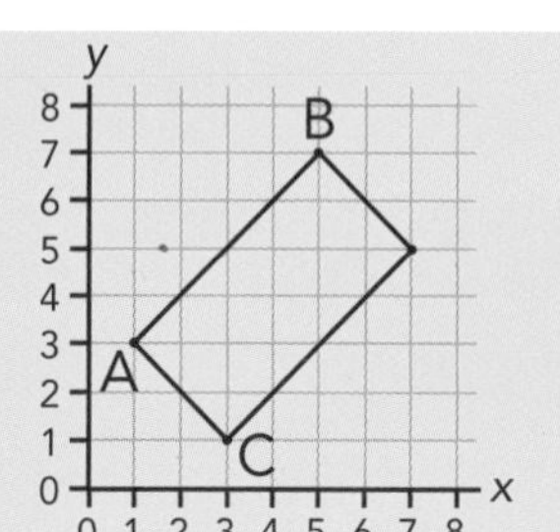

5. Check where the new point is. — **The lines cross at (7, 5) so that is the fourth point.**

Practice question

Write the coordinates of a fourth point that makes a square.

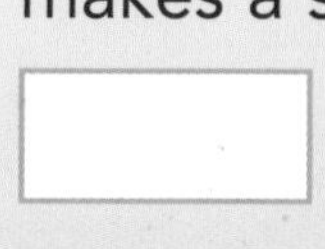

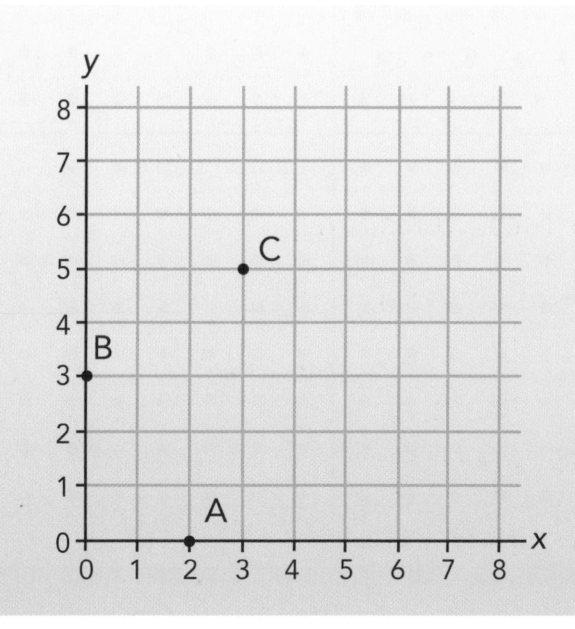

2-D shapes

To achieve Level 4 you need to know all about 2-D shapes, including triangles and rectangles. You also need to know how to draw them on grids.

Triangles

All triangles have 3 sides but there are different types of triangle!

equilateral

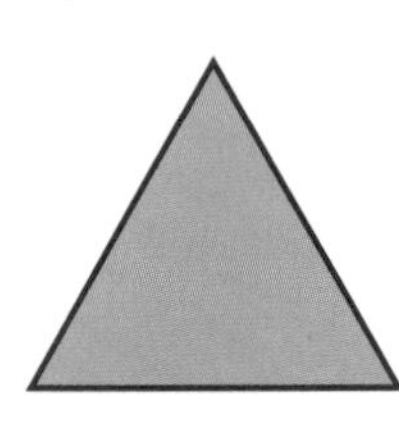

All 3 sides are of equal length.
All 3 angles are equal in size.

isosceles

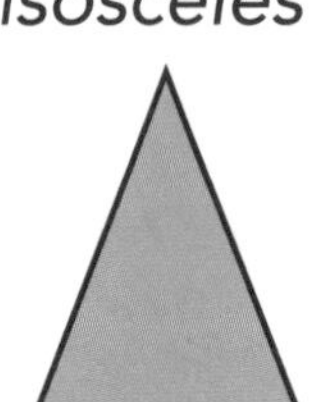

2 sides are equal.
2 angles are equal.

scalene

No sides or angles are equal.

right-angled triangle

One of the angles is a right angle.

A right-angled triangle can be isosceles or scalene.

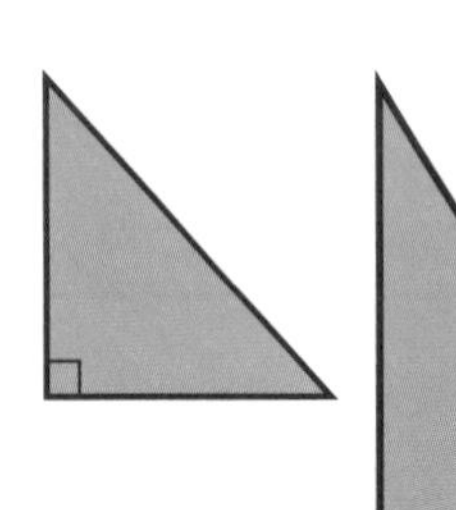

Use these grids to draw three examples of each type of triangle.
Make sure the points (or vertices) of each shape are on the dots.

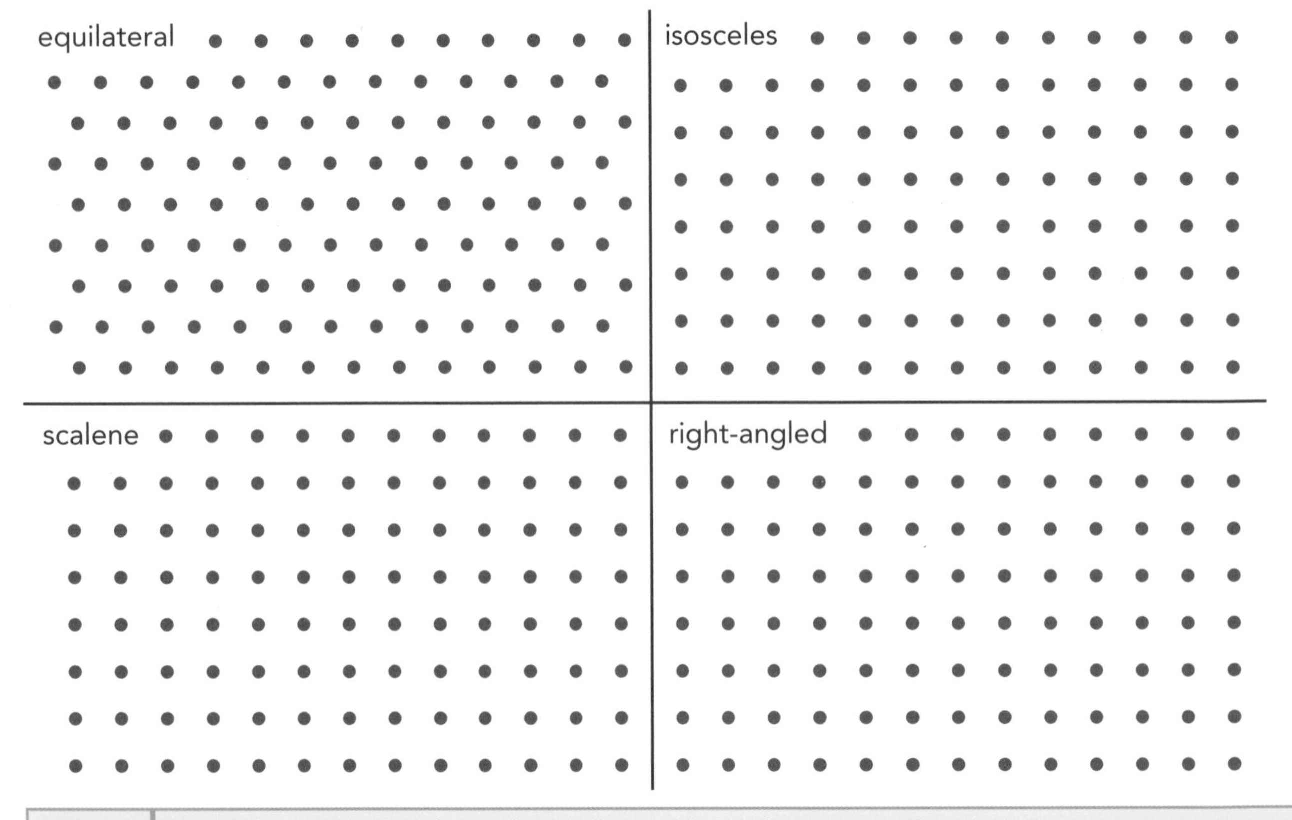

Tip ★ **Use a sharp pencil and a ruler for this exercise and make sure you have these for your test!**

Properties of other 2-D shapes

Achieved?

To achieve Level 4 there are other things about 2-D shapes you need to learn.

Parallel sides

Two lines that are always the same distance apart are called parallel lines.

Think of railway lines – they **must** be parallel for a train to stay on the track.

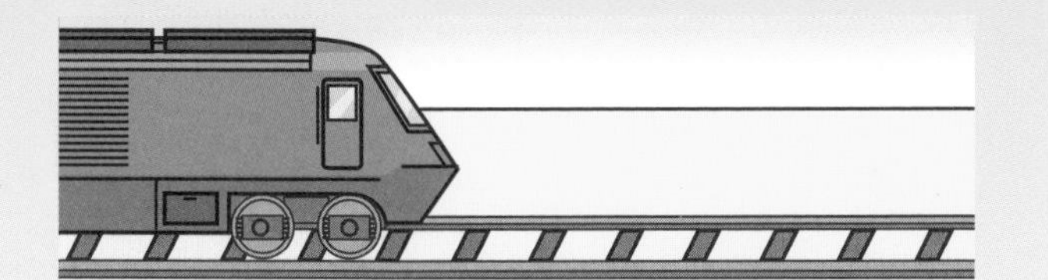

Perpendicular lines

Two straight lines that make a right angle when they cross are called perpendicular lines.

Rectangles

It is important to learn and remember these properties of a rectangle.

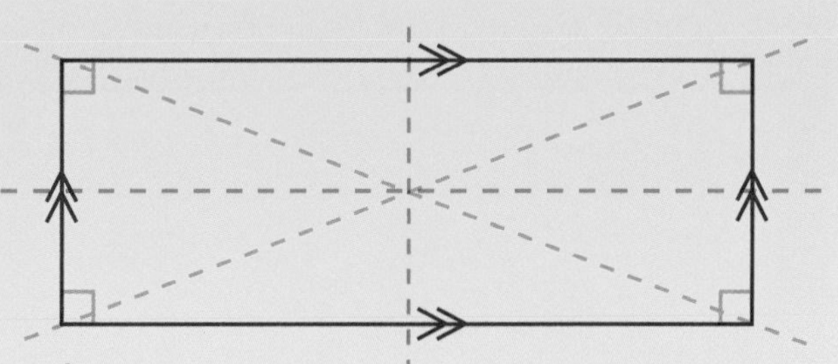

a) All four angles are right angles.

b) The opposite sides are parallel and equal.

c) The diagonals bisect each other (dashed blue lines on the diagram).

d) There are two lines of symmetry (dashed red lines on the diagram).

Parallel Lines that never meet and are always the same distance from one another are parallel. This symbol shows when two lines are parallel ≪ .

Bisect This means that when lines cross they cut each other in half.

Square A rectangle with four equal sides!

Practice activities

1. Draw 3 rectangles of different sizes.
   - Use a protractor to draw the angles accurately.
   - Use a ruler to draw the sides accurately.

2. For each rectangle:
   - Mark two pairs of parallel lines.
   - Label the length of each side.
   - Draw in the lines of symmetry.
   - Draw one diagonal and measure its length.

3-D shapes

To get a Level 4 you have to be able to imagine what a 3-D shape would look like if it was 'unfolded' – that is, when it is a 'net'.

The net of a solid shape is what it looks like when it has been opened out and laid flat.

Imagine unfolding a box of coloured pencils so that the box is just one flat piece of card.

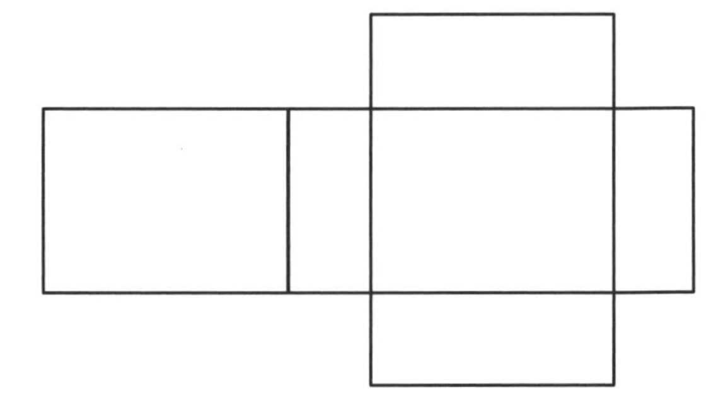

Practice questions

1. Can you link the nets to the 3-D shapes? Draw a line to match them up. Try to picture the nets folding themselves up in front of your eyes. Imagination is important in maths, you know!

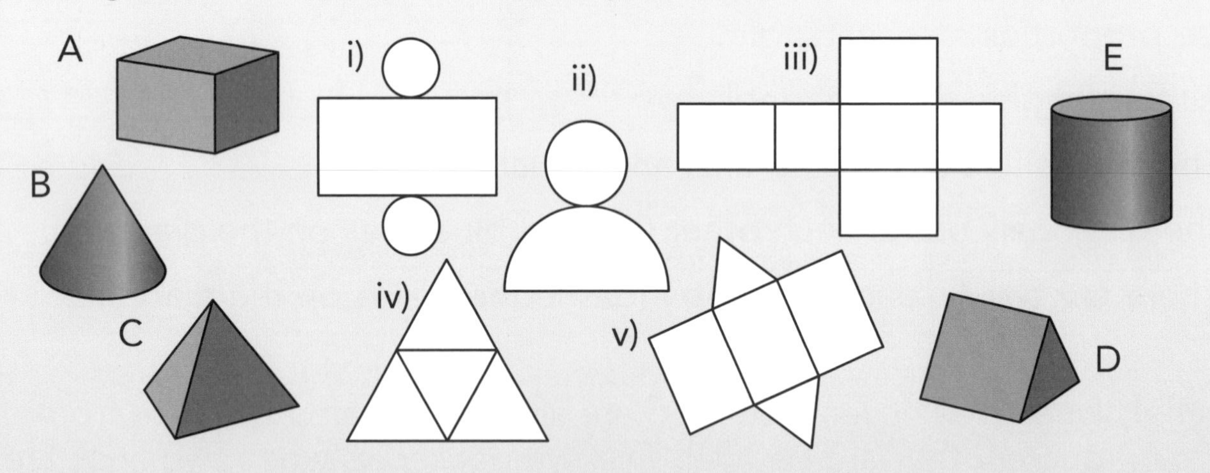

2. Some shapes, like the cube, have more than one net. Can you see which of these nets would form a cube? Circle them.

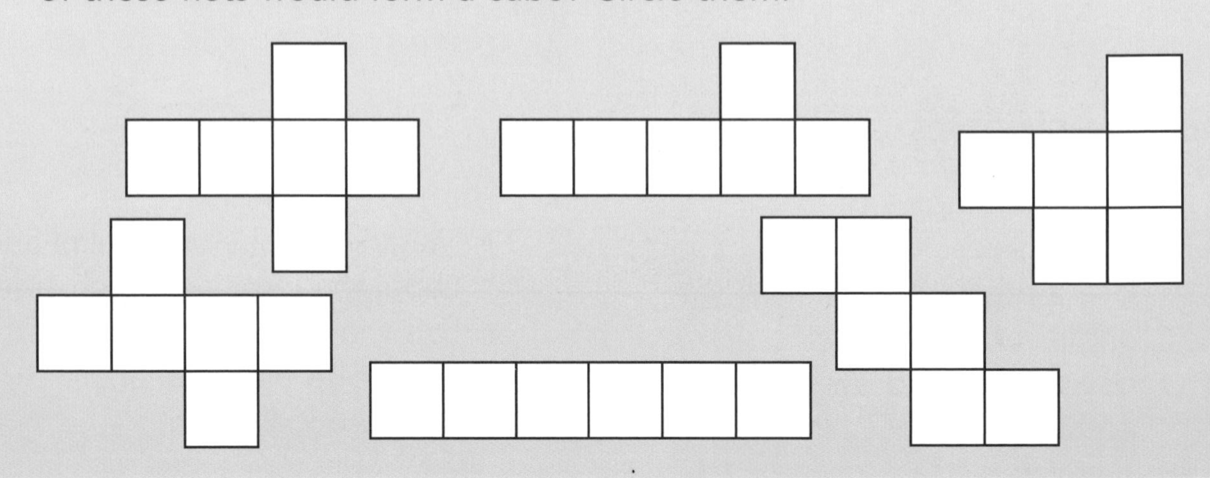

Completing a 3-D shape

A popular question is to ask you to visualise 3-D shapes that have blocks missing.

Let's practise!

What is the smallest number of blocks needed to turn this shape into a cuboid?

1	Read the question then read it again.	What are you being asked to do?
2	Picture the complete shape in your head.	What would it look like? Think about each block. Don't forget to include the blocks you can't see.
3	Work out the dimensions of the shape.	'Dimensions' means how many blocks long, wide and high it is. This shape is 4 blocks long, 4 blocks wide and 3 blocks high.
4	Calculate how many blocks are in each layer.	There should be $4 \times 4 = 16$ blocks in each layer. There are 3 layers. $3 \times 16 = 48$. Cool!
5	Count how many blocks are missing from each layer to get your answer.	Bottom layer: 3 missing Middle layer: 5 missing Top layer: 9 missing $3 + 5 + 9 = 17$ blocks missing
6	Does your answer look right? If not, go back to step 1.	Yes, it does. We need 17 blocks to turn the shape into a cuboid.

Practice questions

How many blocks would it take to make these into cuboids?

1

2

Angles

To achieve Level 4 you need to understand about angles. They are measured in degrees. A right angle is 90 degrees (90°).

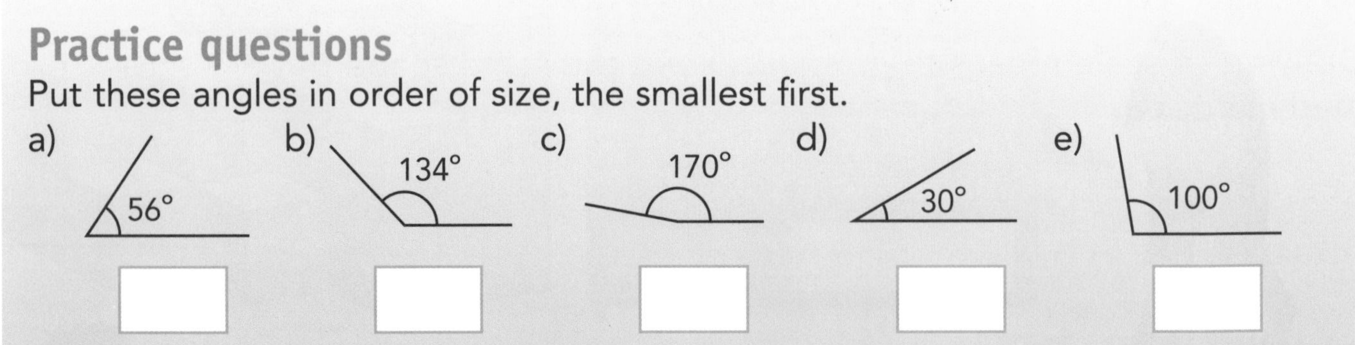

You need to measure angles with a protractor.

Let's practise!

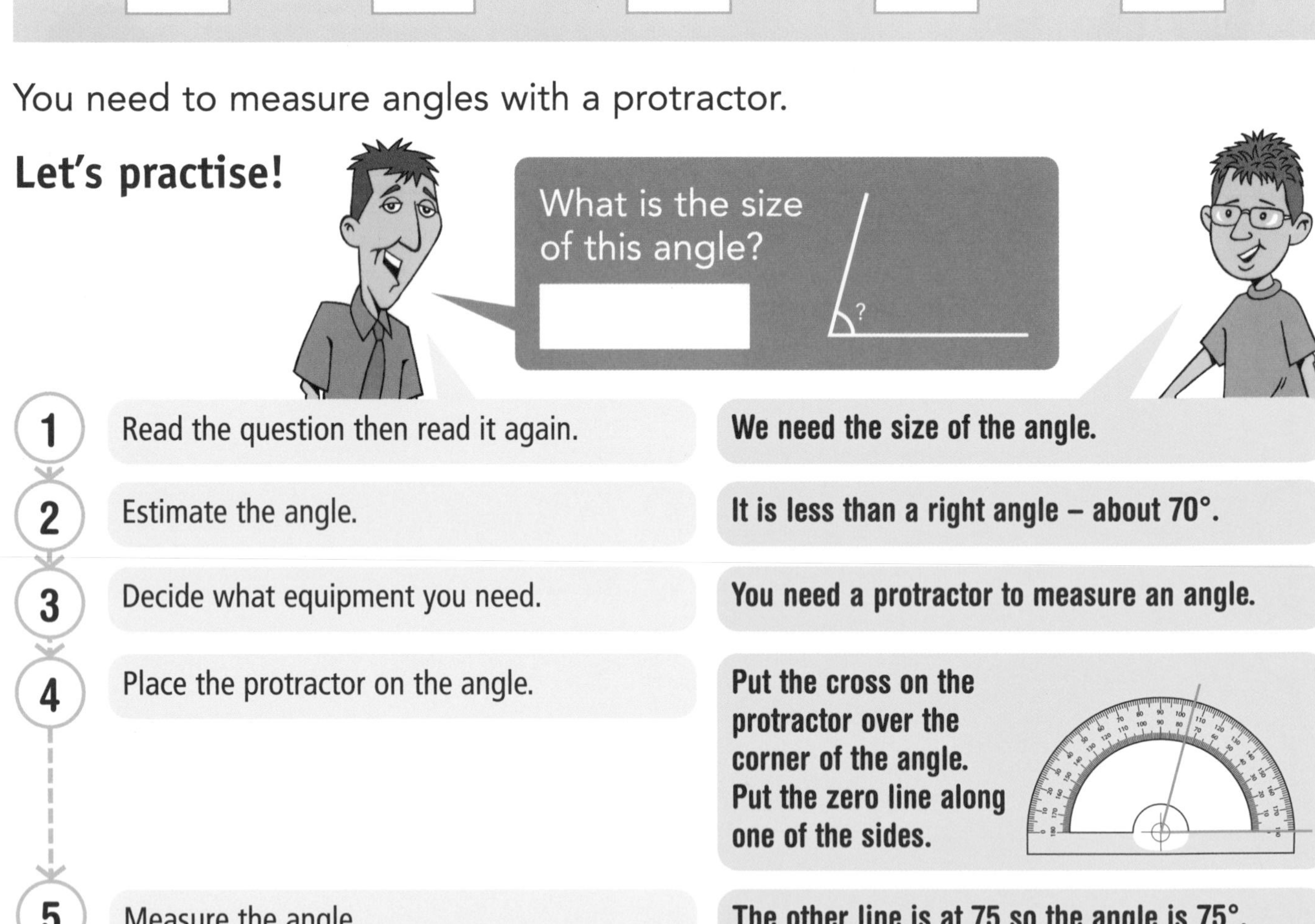

1	Read the question then read it again.	**We need the size of the angle.**
2	Estimate the angle.	**It is less than a right angle – about 70°.**
3	Decide what equipment you need.	**You need a protractor to measure an angle.**
4	Place the protractor on the angle.	**Put the cross on the protractor over the corner of the angle. Put the zero line along one of the sides.**
5	Measure the angle.	**The other line is at 75 so the angle is 75°.**
6	Does your answer look sensible?	**Yes, it is a little less than a right angle.**

Tip ★ **Count round the scale from 0.**

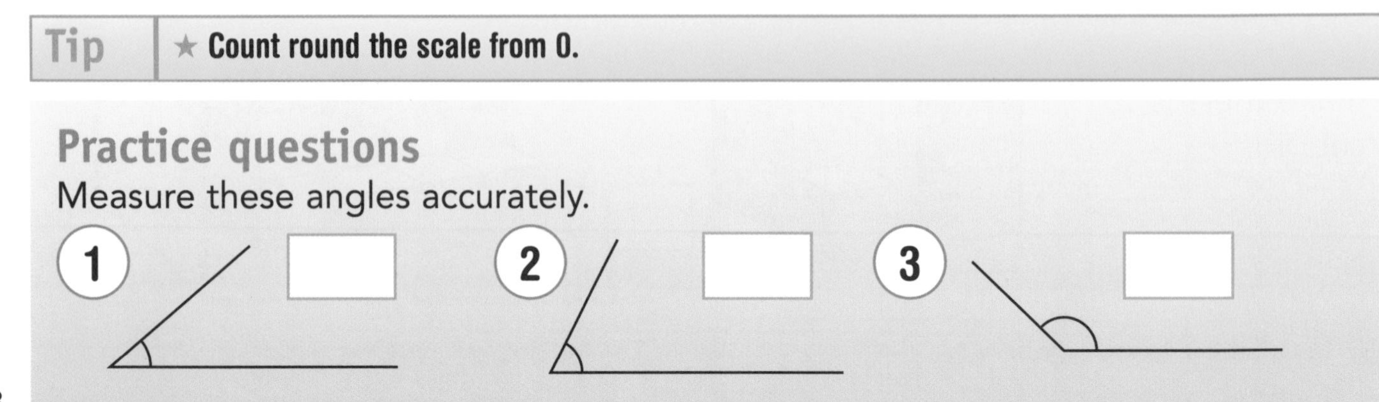

Drawing 2-D and 3-D shapes to scale

Achieved?

To achieve Level 4 you need to be able to draw shapes to scale.

Drawing to scale means that objects keep the same shape but are shrunk or made larger.

Let's practise!

A box is 120 cm by 40 cm by 60 cm.

60 cm

40 cm

120 cm

Use the grid to make a scale drawing, using 1 cm for every 20 cm.

1. Read the question then read it again.
2. Work out the length you need to make each side.

It's 1 cm for every 20 cm.
So 120 cm ÷ 20 = 6 cm
40 cm ÷ 20 = 2 cm
60 cm ÷ 20 = 3 cm

3. Draw the shape onto the grid.

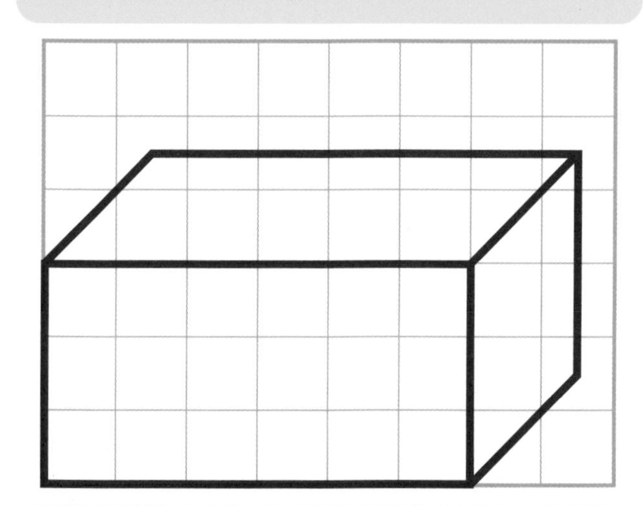

4. Check your measurements.

The lengths are the same as in Step 2.

Moving 2-D shapes

Reflections of simple shapes in a mirror line

To achieve Level 4 you need to be able to reflect a shape in a mirror line placed at any angle.

Let's practise!

Draw a reflection of this shape in the mirror line.

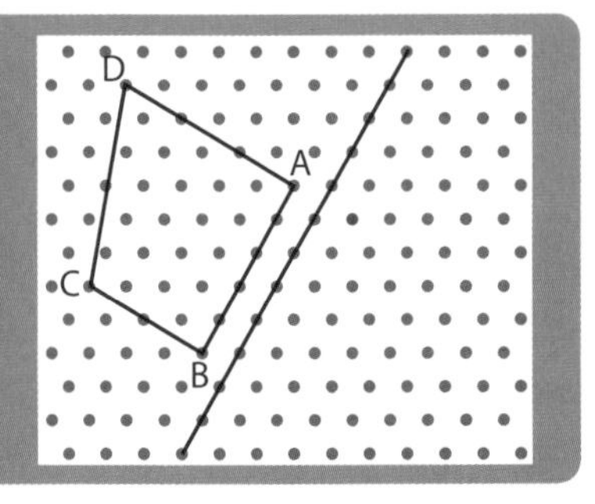

1. Read the question then read it again. — **We need to reflect the shape in the mirror line.**
2. Place a mirror on the mirror line. — **Use the mirror to see its reflection.**
3. Draw the corners of the reflected shape. — **Count the spots from point A to the mirror line and move that number of spots from the line in the opposite direction.**

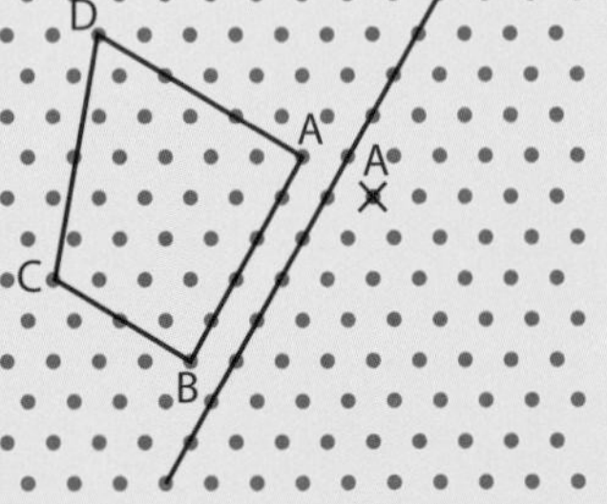

Repeat with the other corners.

4. Complete the shape. — **Use a ruler to join the points.**

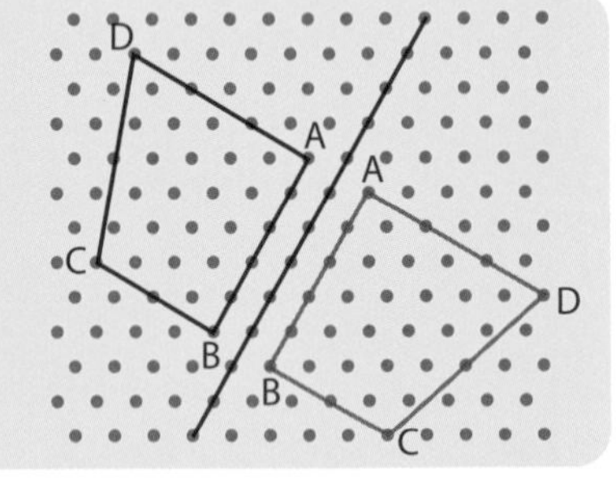

5. Check your answer. — **Make sure the shape you have drawn is in the same position as the one in the mirror and is a 'flipped over' version of the original shape.**

Practice questions

Now try these reflections in the mirror lines.

1 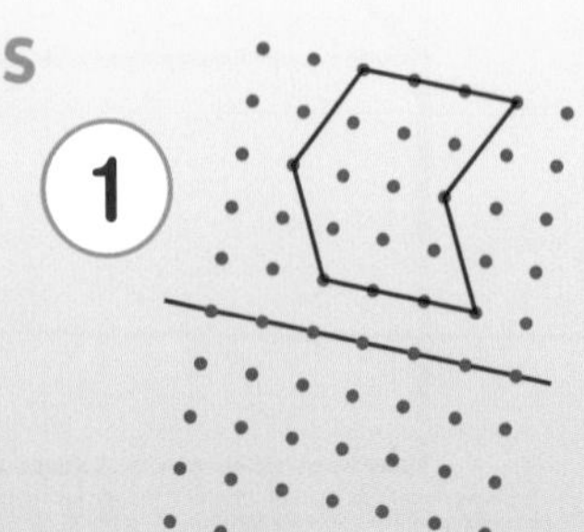

2 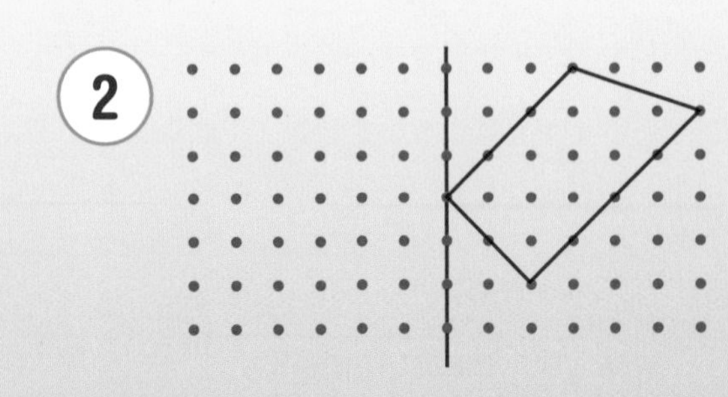

Rotational symmetry

To achieve Level 4 you also need to understand rotational symmetry. Remember, 'rotate' just means turn. It's easy to turn a shape around!

Let's practise!

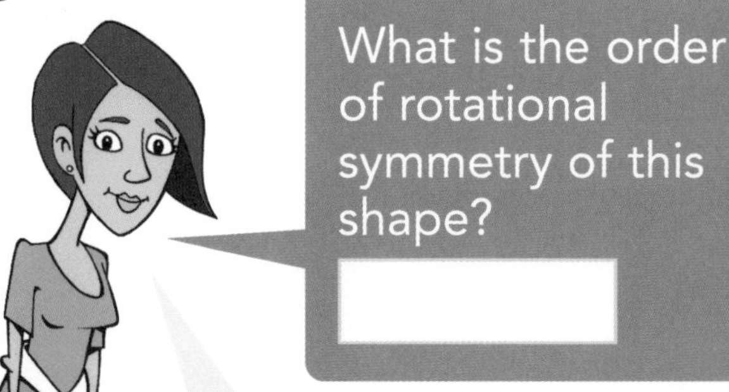

What is the order of rotational symmetry of this shape?

1. Read the question then read it again.

'Rotate' means turn – we need to see how many times we can turn the shape around so that it fits on itself.

2. Trace the shape and mark a starting point X and the centre.

3. Find the order of rotational symmetry.

Fix the tracing paper at the centre and turn it to see how many times the shape will cover itself EXACTLY before the X is back where it started.

4. Check your answer and write it in the answer box.

It fitted 8 times, so it has rotational symmetry of order 8.

Practice questions

1. Write the order of rotational symmetry of these shapes:

a) 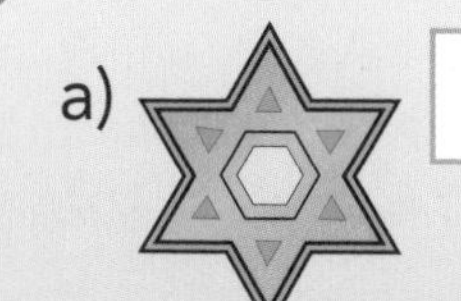

b) 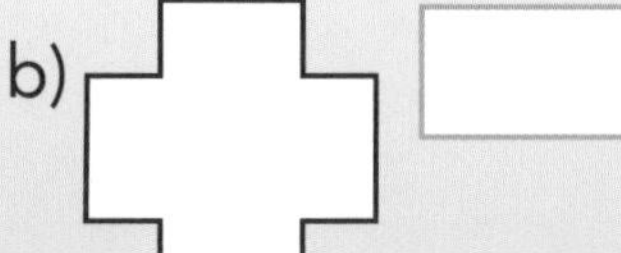

c) 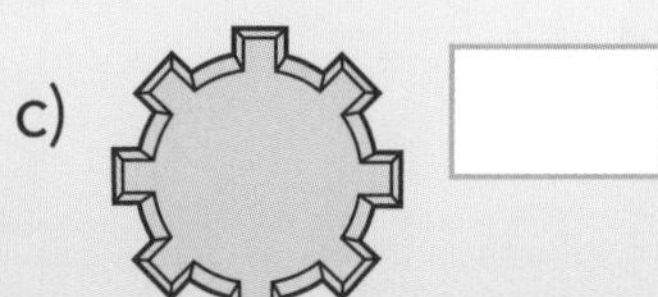

2. Rotate this shape clockwise once through a right angle about A.

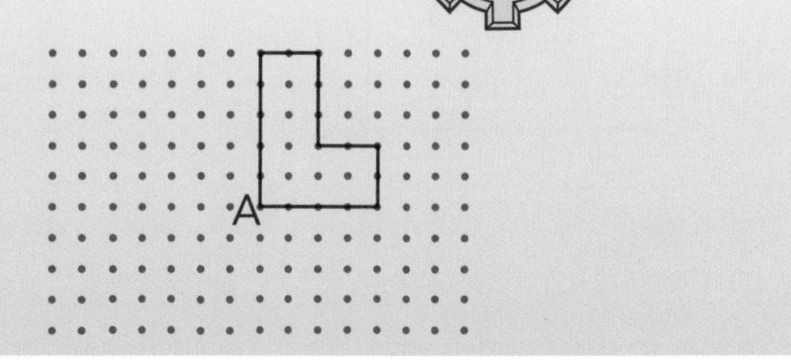

Tip	★ ***Order*** **of rotational symmetry means** ***the number of times*** **you can turn a shape so it fits exactly on top of itself.**

Perimeters of simple shapes

To achieve Level 4 you need to know how to work out the perimeter of a shape. The perimeter of a shape is the distance all the way around its edge.

Let's practise!

What is the perimeter of this rectangle?

1	Read the question then read it again.	**'Perimeter of'. We are being asked to measure the distance around the shape.**
2	First, work out the length of the sides.	**This is the important part! Measure accurately and write on the sides as you work them out. The longer sides are 6.2 cm and the shorter sides are 2.8 cm.**
3	Add up all the lengths.	**6.2 cm + 6.2 cm + 2.8 cm + 2.8 cm = 18 cm**
4	Does your answer look sensible?	**The perimeter of the shape is 18 cm.**

Practice questions

Find the perimeter of these shapes.

1

2

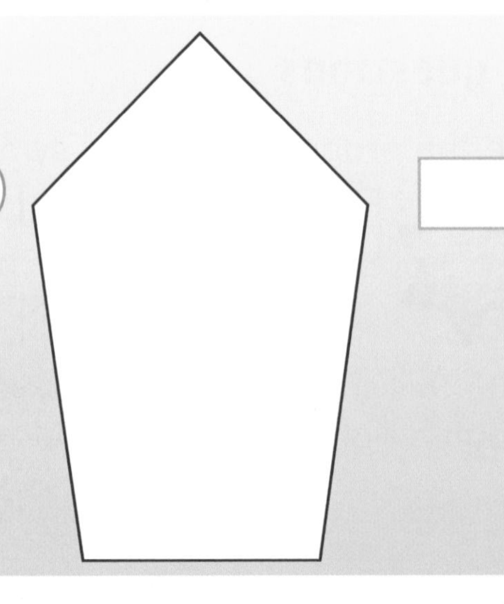

Tips	★ **Be accurate with your measurements. Make sure the start of the line is on the zero on your ruler.**	★ **To remember what perimeter means think of a perimeter fence, which goes ALL THE WAY ROUND a building like a prison or a military base.**

Areas of simple shapes

To achieve Level 4 you need to be able to find the areas of simple shapes.

The area of a shape is the amount of the surface it covers.

We think of the surface as being covered in squares.

Make sure the units you write are always squared, e.g. cm^2 or m^2.

Let's practise!

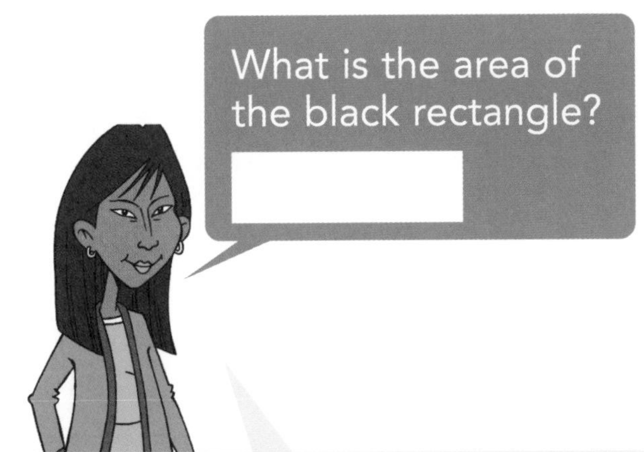

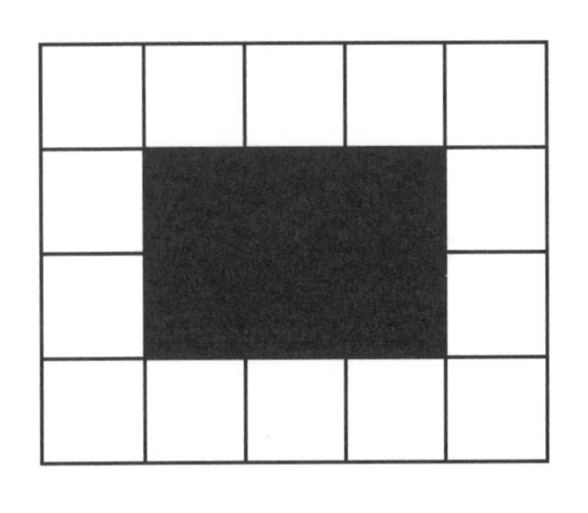

1	Read the question then read it again.	**We have to find the area.**
2	Think of a method to use.	**We need to know how many squares are covered.**
3	Count how many squares are covered.	**There are 2 rows of 3 squares under the shape. That makes 6 squares altogether.**
4	Check if the answer is sensible.	**The answer looks about right.**
5	Write the answer with the units.	**6 cm^2**

Practice questions

Find the area of these shapes.

a)

b)

c)

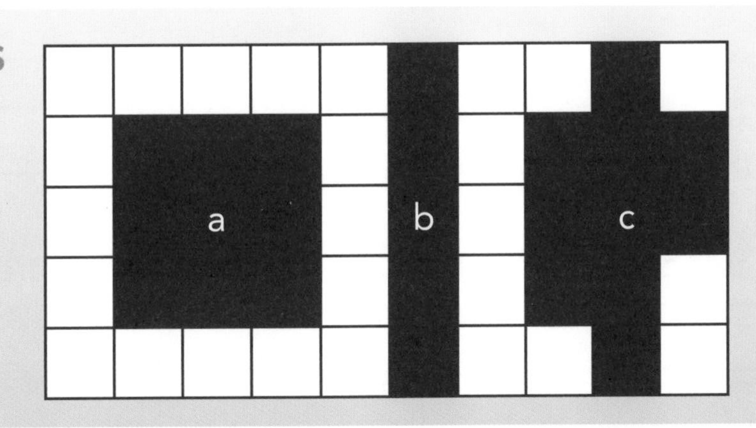

Tip ★ **You can trace the lines on to the shape to make it easy to count the squares.**

Measures

To achieve Level 4 it is important that you know the following things about measures.

- Which units of measure to use when measuring length, mass and capacity.
- Which instruments to use when measuring length, mass and capacity.
- How to read those instruments.

Use the table on this page to learn about the first two!

	Length			Mass (weight)			Capacity		
	Unit	**Instrument**	**Example**	**Unit**	**Instrument**	**Example**	**Unit**	**Instrument**	**Example**
Small size	mm	Ruler	Raisin Sunflower seed	g	Scales	Newspaper Chocolate bar	ml	Teaspoon	Bottle of food colouring for cakes
Medium size	cm	Ruler Metre rule	DVD case Your foot	kg	Bathroom scales	A bag of cement Yourself	l	Measuring jug	Can of cola Glass of milk
Large size	m km	Tape measure Metre wheel	Distance you can ride a bike	kg tonne	Large scales Weigh bridge	Rhinoceros Tractor	l	Container of known capacity	Fish tank Paddling pool

Here are some questions about the table.

1. Name something you would measure in centimetres.
2. Name something you would measure in litres.
3. What instrument would you use to measure the weight of the newspaper?
4. What instrument would you use to measure the length of a sunflower seed?
5. Think of two things not in the table you could measure in:

   a) kg

   b) l

   c) km

Reading scales

Achieved?

At Level 4 it is important that you understand how to read measuring instruments, most of which use scales. The scale can go up in different amounts on different measuring instruments.

Let's practise!

1. Read the question then read it again. — **We are dealing with measures so we need to be accurate.**
2. Think about the numbers. — **The numbers go up in 100s.**
3. Check the unit on the scale. — **The scale is marked in grams (g).**
4. If the measurement is at a numbered mark, read it carefully. — **It is between 200 g and 300 g.**
5. If the measurement is between numbers, work out what each mark is worth and count forwards or backwards. — **Each 100 g is split into 4 sections. 100 g ÷ 4 = 25 g so each section is 25 g. 200 g + 1 mark = 200 g + 25 g = 225 g.**
6. Is your answer sensible? — **The pointer is just past 200 g, so 225 g is sensible.**

Practice question

What is the length of the car?

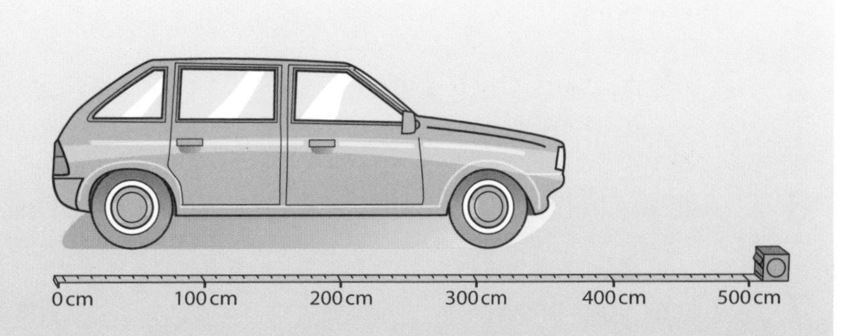

Time and timetables

At Level 4 you may have to read timetables and work out time intervals.

Let's practise!

This is the timetable for Year 6's walking day out.

How long after the start of the walk is the arrival in Furness Vale?

Event	Time
Leave school and start walking	9:15 a.m.
Arrive at High End Farm	10:00 a.m.
Snack in Whaley Park	11:15 a.m.
Arrive in Furness Vale	12:10 p.m.
Lunch	1:15 p.m.
Table Tennis Tournament	1:50 p.m.
Go to canal	2:25 p.m.
Return to school	3:20 p.m.

1. Read the question then read it again. — **We are looking at the start and at Furness Vale.**
2. Write down the times you need. — **The start is 9:15 a.m. Furness Vale is 12:10 p.m.**
3. Approximate an answer. — **9 a.m. to 12 noon is 3 hours.**
4. Calculate how many hours are between these times.

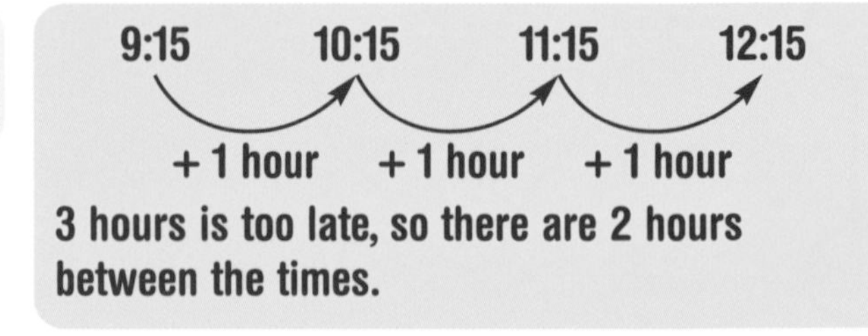

3 hours is too late, so there are 2 hours between the times.

5. Calculate how many minutes are between these times.

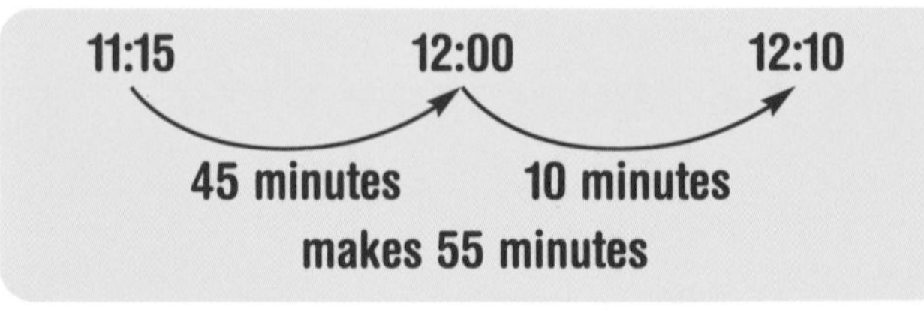

makes 55 minutes

6. Add the hours and minutes. — **That makes 2 hours and 55 minutes.**
7. Check your answer. — **The answer is very close to 3 hours, so it looks like a sensible answer.**

Practice questions

1. How long is it from 8:10 a.m. to 11:45 a.m.?

2. How long is it from 5:20 p.m. to 10:05 p.m.?

3. What time is 4 hours and 40 minutes after 6:10 p.m.?

4. The film 'Callum's Nightmare' starts at 7:20 p.m.

   If it lasts 3 hours and 50 minutes, what time does it end?

5.

Taxal	7:00	7:15	7:40	7:55
Moorside	7:15	7:30	7:55	
Disley	7:22	7:37	8:02	

   a) Georgia needs to be at Disley at 10 to 8.

   What time should she catch the bus from Taxal?

   b) Complete the times in the last column of the bus timetable.

6. It takes Alex 25 minutes to walk from home to school.

   a) If he sets off at 8:30 a.m., what time will he arrive at school?

   b) At the end of the day Alex leaves school at 3:40 p.m.

   At what time will he get home?

   c) Alex walks to school and back every day for 5 days.

   How many hours and minutes does he spend walking?

   hours and minutes

7. It takes Rachel 3 hours and 20 minutes to cycle from her house to her cousin's house. If she needs to be there at ¼ past 2 in the afternoon, what is the latest time she can leave home?

Tips

- ★ **Check carefully whether the time crosses the hour.**
- ★ **Notice which times are a.m. and which are p.m. It can make a big difference to the answer!**

Line graphs

Line graphs are an important part of Level 4. A graph with **time** on the **x** axis (horizontal) and **numbers** on the **y** axis (vertical) often shows a set of points joined by a line. Only the points have a value – the line between just shows the trend.

Here is a line graph showing the number of visitors to 'Rally Road' go-kart arena over the course of a year.

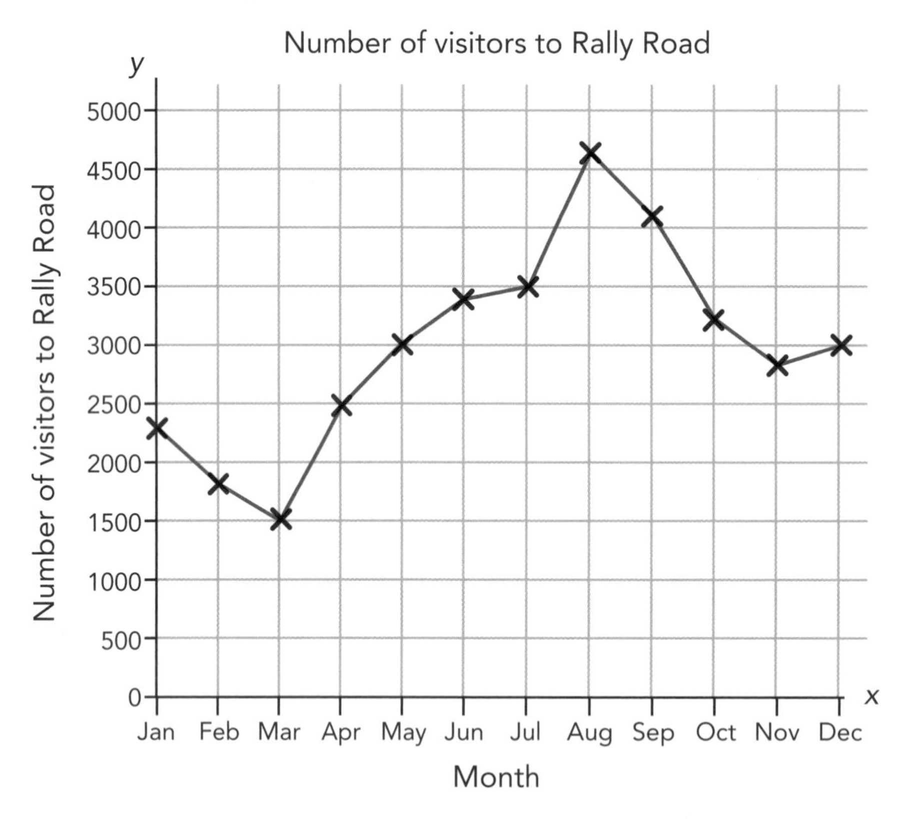

Try answering these questions.

1. a) Which was the least popular month? ____

   b) How many visitors did Rally Road have in that month? ____

2. The number of visitors first fell between ____ and ____.

3. In which month were there 2800 visitors? ____

4. Why do you think there were most visitors in August?

   ____

5. How many visitors do you think there were in June? ____

Tip	★ **When reading graphs, make sure you follow the lines carefully across and up and down. Using a ruler can help.**

Let's practise!

Buxworth School's lacrosse team kept a record of the number of goals they scored every day in a week-long tournament. Can you display this information on a line graph?

Day	Mon	Tues	Wed	Thurs	Fri	Sat	Sun
Number of goals	3	5	9	14	9	13	17

1. Read the question then read it again. — **You need to draw a line graph.**
2. Decide which information fits on each axis. — **The days (time) should go on the *x* axis and the goals scored (number) should go on the *y* axis.**
3. Decide on a scale. — **We need a scale for the number of goals. The highest number is 17 and our grid is 10 squares high – we need to go up in steps of 2.**
4. Plot the points. — **This must be accurate. Start at Monday on the *x* axis and work along to Sunday.**
5. Join the points to show the trend. — **Does it match the results table?**

Put the information on the graph using the flow chart to help you.

Then answer the questions below.

1. On how many days did Buxworth School score more than 8 goals? ______

2. Between which two days did their score improve the most?

   ______ and ______

3. a) What was the general trend over the week for the number of goals scored?

   ______

   b) Which day was different to the general trend? ______

Tip ★ **Always use a sharp pencil when plotting points – it helps you to be more accurate.**

Grouping data

To achieve Level 4 you need to know about grouped data graphs.

Here is a chart showing the number of questions answered correctly by 16 children in a school quiz with 30 questions. We wanted to find out how many children scored between 16 and 20 marks.

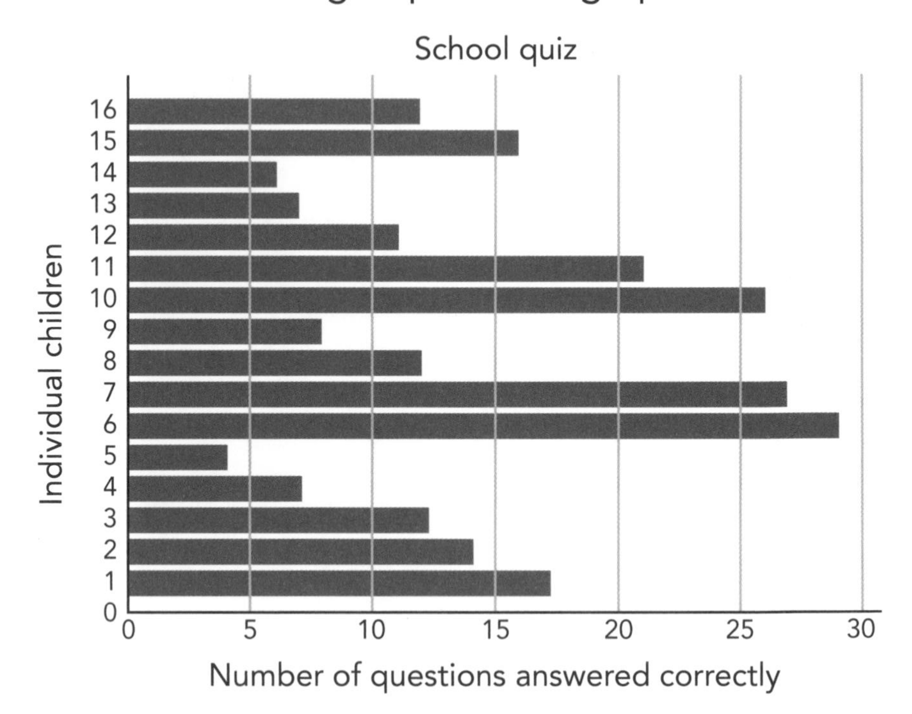

This looks quite complicated! We can make it easier if we group the scores and then compare them.

Look at the new chart and answer the questions below.

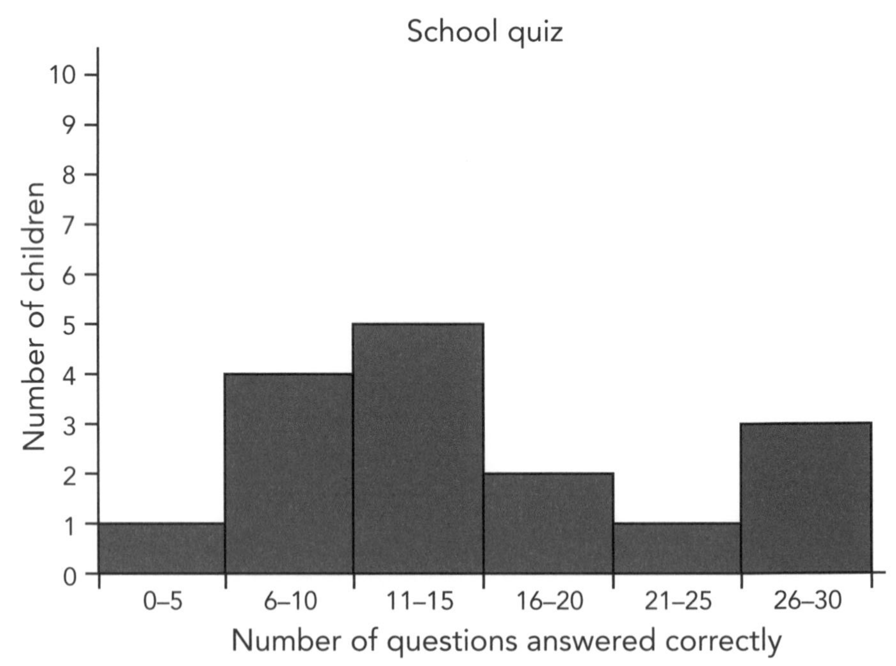

Questions

1. How many children scored between 16 and 20 marks?
2. How many children scored more than 15 marks?
3. What was the second most common range of scores in the quiz?
4. How many children scored fewer than 21 marks?
5. Look at both of the charts. Did anyone get all the questions right?

A week later some children answered the same questions again. Their scores had improved! Here are the results. Can you draw a bar chart and group the data? Are most scores still between 11 and 15?

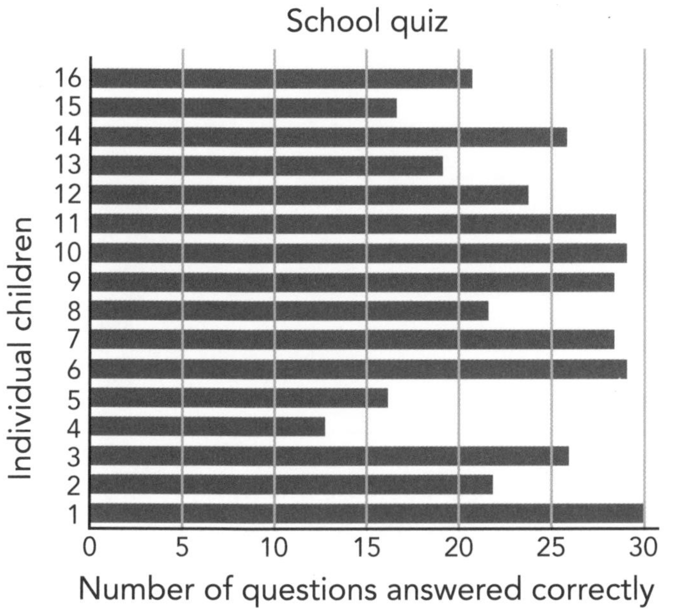

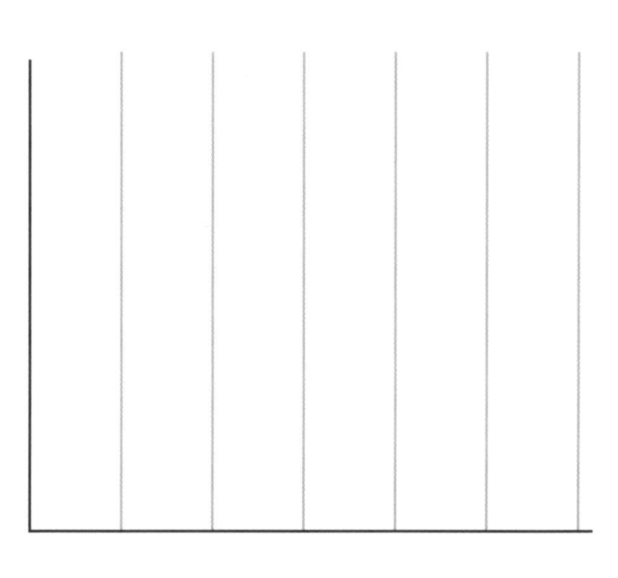

1. Read the question then read it again.

… draw the chart and find the most common score …

2. Group the data in equal amounts. Mark on your axis.

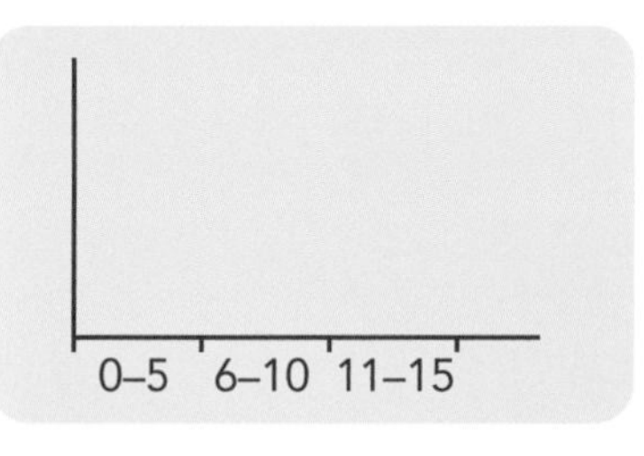

3. Tally the number for each group of data.

OK. The first group is 0–5. How many children scored 0–5? None. Now the next group. None again. Now the 11–15 group. Ah! 1. Next the 16–20 group … 3. Next the 21–25 group … 4. Finally the 26–30 group … 8.

4. Draw in the bars.

The most common score is now between 26 and 30.

5. Check your results. Do they look sensible?

Yes, the children scored much higher. This looks right.

Tips	★ **Think clearly. Work step by step.**	★ **When handling data, a rough piece of paper can be useful to make notes or tally information.**

Finding the range and mode

To achieve Level 4 you need to understand the range and mode.

Let's practise!

These are the ages of the Bright Stars football team.

18 22 23 29 22 18 29 23 22 23 22

What are the range and mode of these ages?

1. Read the question then read it again.
2. Think about the question.

   The range is the difference between the highest and lowest numbers.
   The mode is the most common value.
3. Calculate the range.

   The highest number is 29.
   The lowest number is 18.
   The range is 29 – 18 = 11
4. Find the mode.

   Make sets of the same number.

18	22	23	29
18	22	23	29
	22	23	
	22		

   22 occurs most often so 22 is the mode.
5. If your answer looks sensible, write it in the box. If not, go back to step 2 and try again.

Practice question

Ben counts how many people log on to his website every day for 2 weeks.

20 13 32 20 35 20 25 13 30 62 13 24 13 23

What is the range and mode for the number of hits?

Tips

- ★ **Scan the list and mark the lowest number.**
- ★ **Check through the list to see if it really is the lowest. Repeat for the highest number.**
- ★ **Remember:**
  - **Mode is the most common value.**
  - **Modal means mode.**
- ★ **Always write out the numbers again and sort them. Tick off each number so you know you haven't missed any of them. This is IMPORTANT!**

Using and applying mathematics

To achieve Level 4 you need to be able to solve all kinds of maths problems.

The reason for learning all the different mathematical skills (multiplying, dividing, measuring, estimating and so on) is so you can use them to solve mathematical problems.

Imagine learning all the shots in tennis – like the serve, the volley, the backhand and forehand – but never actually getting to play a game! Only by using your shots in a match will you learn to be a tennis player. Likewise, only by using your mathematical skills will you learn to be a mathematician!

The flow chart on page 54 is designed to guide you when tackling a maths problem. It will help organise your thinking, but it won't tell you the answer – that's for you to work out for yourself.

The next few pages contain problems for you to solve. Work through the examples first and then have a go at the practice questions using the flow chart approach.

Good luck!

Problem solving

Number

These questions are all about your number skills. You must use them in the right way though!

Shape and space

These questions all require you to use your knowledge about shapes, both 2-D and 3-D.

Measures

These questions are all about real situations: going on a journey, the amount of milk a family drinks in a week and so on.

Handling data

These questions often ask you to find out information from a table or chart. They will also ask you to explain how you found out the answer!

The problem-solving flow chart

1	Read the question then read it again.	**Read the question twice carefully. Let the words and numbers 'sink in'.**
2	Write the numbers and highlight any key words.	**Write down any numbers and key words. It might help to draw a picture or diagram.**
3	Can you estimate an answer?	**This depends on the question. Try to estimate using the numbers and words you jotted down in step 2.**
4	Which calculations do you need to do?	**Work out if you need to use +, −, × or ÷. Check if you need to do more than one calculation.**
5	Work out the problem.	**Do any calculations needed. Make sure you are answering the problem.**
6	Is your answer sensible?	**Read the question again and check that your answer is realistic. If not, go back to step 2.**

Tips

- ★ **Remember your 'checking the answer' skills.**
- ★ **Think clearly and write clearly.**
- ★ **Present your work so it shows what you have done.**
- ★ **Work step by step.**
- ★ **Make a problem easier (e.g. 'Find 24 lots of 6.' Try finding 4 lots first, then 20 lots).**
- ★ **Take a reasonable guess at what you think might happen.**
- ★ **Think HOW you are working. Change your method if something isn't working.**
- ★ **Look for patterns in your maths.**

Number patterns

Achieved?

Number patterns or sequences are lists of numbers that follow a pattern. To achieve Level 4 you need to work out a sequence by finding the difference between the numbers.

Let's practise!

Fill in the missing numbers and explain the rule in writing.

27, 40, ☐, ☐, 79

1. Read the question then read it again.
   There are two parts to this question. Don't forget the second part.
2. Picture the numbers.
   Starting at 27 and going upwards towards 79.
3. Look at the difference between the first two numbers that are next to each other.
   27 and 40. The difference is 13.
4. Use the difference you have found and 'test it' on the sequence.
   40 + 13 = 53
   53 + 13 = 66
   66 + 13 = 79 It fits!
5. If it fits the sequence, fill in your answer and explain the rule.
   Fill in the boxes correctly.
   53 66
   Explain the rule: 'Add 13 each time.'

Practice questions

Try to fill in the gaps to complete these sequences. Explain the rule you find.

1. 8, 14, ☐, 26, ☐ ______________________
2. 9, ☐, ☐, 0, –3 ______________________
3. ☐, 78, 99, ☐, ☐ ______________________

Solving number problems

Achieved?

To achieve Level 4 you have to solve number problems that need more than one calculation.

The numbers in row 2 of this triangle of snooker balls have been found from the two numbers directly above them using a rule. Fill in the missing numbers and write the rule.

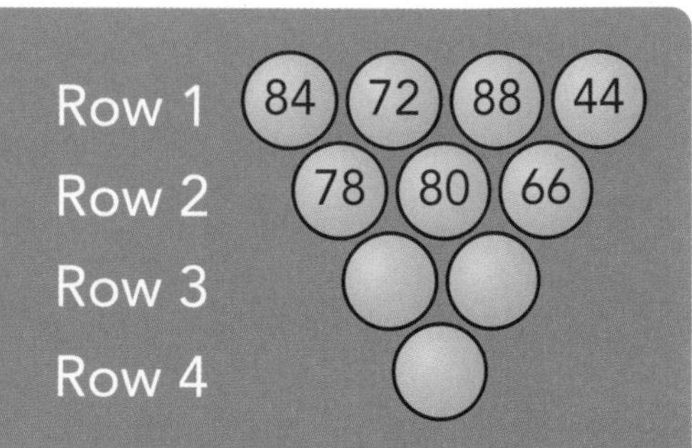

Rule:

1	Read the question then read it again.	**There are two things to do in this question – 'find the missing numbers' and 'write the rule'.**
2	Write the numbers and highlight any key words.	**'Numbers in row 2'; 'found from the two numbers directly above'. How do 84 and 72 make 78?**
3	Can you estimate an answer?	**No, because the answer is not obvious.**
4	Which calculations do you need to do?	**Work step by step. What do we have to do to get 78? Perhaps 84 + 72 or 84 – 72?**
5	Work out the problem.	**84 + 72 = 156 and 84 – 72 = 12 Look at our answers. Can we see any link with 78? Yes! 78 is half of 156. The answer is 'add the two numbers and divide the answer by 2'. Now we can fill in the other missing numbers. (78 + 80) ÷ 2 = 79; (80 + 66) ÷ 2 = 73; (79 + 73) ÷ 2 = 76**
6	Is your answer sensible?	**Yes. We applied our rule and it worked!**

Solving measures problems

Achieved?

To achieve Level 4 you need to use your knowledge of measures when solving problems.

Here is a list of ingredients for banana mousse.

It feeds 4 people.

1.2 kg bananas	6 eggs
300 ml milk	4 tablespoons sugar

Gordon wants to prepare banana mousse for 6 people. Can you change the amount of each ingredient so he makes enough mousse? Show your method:

1	Read the question then read it again.	**Change the amounts of the four ingredients.**
2	Write the numbers and highlight any key words.	**4 people to 6 people. Ah! That's an increase of half as much again or 50%.**
3	Can you estimate an answer?	**We can easily work out that we need $6 + (\frac{1}{2}$ of $6) = 9$ eggs and $4 + 2 = 6$ tablespoons of sugar. We can estimate an answer of 1.7 kg of bananas and 500 ml of milk.**
4	Which calculations do you need to do?	**(50% of 1.2 kg) + 1.2 kg (50% of 300 ml) + 300 ml**
5	Work out the problem.	**50% of 1.2 kg = 600 g 1200 g + 600 g = 1800 g or 1.8 kg 50% of 300 ml = 150 ml 300 ml + 150 ml = 450 ml**
6	Is your answer sensible?	**Gordon would need 1.8 kg of bananas, 450 ml of milk, 9 eggs and 6 tablespoons of sugar. Those look like sensible amounts for mousse for 6 people!**

Solving shape problems

To achieve Level 4 you need to use your knowledge about shape when solving problems.

How many rectangles can you see in this shape?

Show your method:

1. Read the question then read it again.

   Study the words. Study the shape. Think past 'the obvious'.

2. Write the numbers and highlight any key words.

   'How many'? We are going to need the *total* number of rectangles. Think how you could work in a logical step-by-step way.

3. Can you estimate an answer?

   We can see 9 inside the big one straight away. That's 10. Let's double that. 20? We can only guess.

4. Which calculations do you need to do?

   Work in a logical way.
   How many 1 unit rectangles are there?
   How many 2 unit rectangles are there?
   And so on. It might help to use a table.

5. Work out the problem.

Number of units	1	2	3	4	5	6	7	8	9	Total
Number of rectangles	9	12	6	4	0	4	0	0	1	36

There are 36 rectangles in this shape.

6. Is your answer sensible?

   It looks sensible because we worked it out in a step-by-step way.

Solving data handling problems

To achieve Level 4 you need to read information carefully and accurately when solving problems.

Theo has carried out a survey of some popular computer games. Find *Gran Theft Skateboard*, *HALO 5* and *Wrestling Fest* in the Carroll diagram below. Draw a Venn diagram as in the example and write the games on it in the correct place.

	Suitable for ages 12 and under	Not suitable for ages 12 and under
1 player only	*Gran Theft Skateboard* *Speed Racer 2*	*Zombie Hunter* *Horror-shocker*
2 or more players	*Wrestling Fest*	*Car-jacker* *HALO 5*

Example:

Suitable for 12 and under

1 player only

1	Read the question then read it again.	**There are two different diagrams to look at and understand.**
2	Write the numbers and highlight any key words.	**We need to transfer information from one diagram to another. Understanding the Carroll diagram is important, e.g. *Car-jacker* and *HALO 5* are for 2 or more players and are not suitable for ages 12 and under.**
3	Can you estimate an answer?	**No, it would be a wild guess.**
4	Which calculations do you need to do?	**No calculations here. We need to put three games in the correct place on the Venn diagram.**
5	What is the answer to the problem?	***Wrestling Fest* is for ages 12 and under but needs 2 or more players, so write it in the left-hand part of the left circle. *Gran Theft Skateboard* is for 12 and under AND 1 player only, so write it where the two circles overlap. *HALO 5* doesn't fit in either category so write it outside both circles but inside the border of the Venn diagram.**
6	Is your answer sensible?	**After double-checking where we have written each game, it is a sensible answer.**

Check problems by context

To achieve Level 4 you need to know how to check answers to problems by thinking about the problem.

Let's practise!

1	Read the question then read it again.	**Make sure you understand what you are being asked to find out.**
2	Think about the numbers.	**Tickets cost 25p. 500p is the same as £5.**
3	Use the numbers to check the answer.	**4 tickets would cost £1. So £5 would buy 5 x 4 tickets. That's 20 tickets.**
4	Is that the correct answer?	**No – 20 is not close to 200.**

Practice questions

1. Libby has 92 rabbits. She keeps 4 rabbits in each run.
   Tom says she needs 20 runs.

   Is he correct? ☐

   Explain how you know.

   ____

2. Nye can make 5 cubes in 8 minutes.
   George says it would take him 40 minutes to make 21 cubes.

   Is he correct? ☐

   Explain how you know.

   ____

Learning objectives for Primary Mathematics Framework

This table may be useful for your teacher or carer. They can see what you have learnt in Year 5 and what you will be learning in Year 6. They will be able to see your progression for each strand following the Primary Mathematics Framework.

The key objectives are in **bold type**.

Attainment target and Strand	Year 5	Year 6
Using and applying mathematics	Solve one-step and two-step problems involving whole numbers and decimals and all four operations, choosing and using appropriate calculation strategies	Solve multi-step problems, and problems involving fractions, decimals and percentages; choose and use appropriate calculation strategies at each stage
	Represent a puzzle or problem by identifying and recording the information or calculations needed to solve it; find possible solutions and confirm them in the context of the problem	Tabulate systematically the information in a problem or puzzle; identify and record the steps or calculations needed to solve it, using symbols where appropriate; interpret solutions in the original context and check their accuracy
	Plan and pursue an enquiry; present evidence by collecting, organising and interpreting information; suggest extensions to the enquiry	Suggest, plan and develop lines of enquiry; collect, organise and represent information, interpret results and review methods; identify and answer related questions
	Explore patterns, properties and relationships and propose a general statement involving numbers or shapes; identify examples for which the statement is true or false	Represent and interpret sequences, patterns and relationships involving numbers and shapes; suggest and test hypotheses; construct and use simple expressions and formulae in words then symbols (e.g. the cost of c pens at 15 pence each is 15c pence)
	Explain reasoning using diagrams, graphs and text; refine ways of recording using images and symbols	Explain reasoning and conclusions, using words, symbols or diagrams as appropriate
Number and algebra Counting and understanding number	Count from any given number in whole-number and decimal steps, extending beyond zero when counting backwards; relate the numbers to their position on a number line	Find the difference between a positive and a negative integer, or two negative integers, in context
	Explain what each digit represents in whole numbers and decimals with up to two places, and partition, round and order these numbers	Use decimal notation for tenths, hundredths and thousandths; partition, round and order decimals with up to three places, and position them on the number line
	Express a smaller whole number as a fraction of a larger one (e.g. recognise that 5 out of 8 is $\frac{5}{8}$); find equivalent fractions (e.g. $\frac{7}{10} = \frac{14}{20}$, or $\frac{19}{10} = 1\frac{9}{10}$); relate fractions to their decimal representations	Express a larger whole number as a fraction of a smaller one (e.g. recognise that 8 slices of a 5-slice pizza represents $\frac{8}{5}$ or $1\frac{3}{5}$ pizzas); simplify fractions by cancelling common factors; order a set of fractions by converting them to fractions with a common denominator
	Understand percentage as the number of parts in every 100 and express tenths and hundredths as percentages	**Express one quantity as a percentage of another (e.g. express £400 as a percentage of £1000); find equivalent percentages, decimals and fractions**
	Use sequences to scale numbers up or down; solve problems involving proportions of quantities (e.g. decrease quantities in a recipe designed to feed six people)	Solve simple problems involving direct proportion by scaling quantities up or down
Number and algebra Knowing and using number facts	**Use knowledge of place value and addition and subtraction of two-digit numbers to derive sums and differences and doubles and halves of decimals (e.g. 6.5 ± 2.7, half of 5.6, double 0.34)**	**Use knowledge of place value and multiplication facts to 10 × 10 to derive related multiplication and division facts involving decimals (e.g. 0.8 × 7, 4.8 ÷ 6)**
	Recall quickly multiplication facts up to 10 × 10 and use them to multiply pairs of multiples of 10 and 100; derive quickly corresponding division facts	Use knowledge of multiplication facts to derive quickly squares of numbers to 12 × 12 and the corresponding squares of multiples of 10
	Identify pairs of factors of two-digit whole numbers and find common multiples (e.g. for 6 and 9)	Recognise that prime numbers have only two factors and identify prime numbers less than 100; find the prime factors of two-digit numbers
	Use knowledge of rounding, place value, number facts and inverse operations to estimate and check calculations	Use approximations, inverse operations and tests of divisibility to estimate and check results

Attainment target and Strand	Year 5	Year 6
Number and algebra Calculating	Extend mental methods for whole-number calculations, for example to multiply a two-digit by a one-digit number (e.g. 12 × 9), to multiply by 25 (e.g. 16 × 25), to subtract one near multiple of 1000 from another (e.g. 6070 – 4097)	Calculate mentally with integers and decimals: U.t ± U.t, TU × U, TU ÷ U, U.t × U, U.t ÷ U
	Use efficient written methods to add and subtract whole numbers and decimals with up to two places	**Use efficient written methods to add and subtract integers and decimals, to multiply and divide integers and decimals by a one-digit integer, and to multiply two-digit and three-digit integers by a two-digit integer**
	Use understanding of place value to multiply and divide whole numbers and decimals by 10, 100 or 1000	Relate fractions to multiplication and division (e.g. 6 ÷ 2 = ½ of 6 = 6 × ½); express a quotient as a fraction or decimal (e.g. 67 ÷ 5 = 13.4 or 13⅖); find fractions and percentages of whole-number quantities (e.g. ⅝ of 96, 65% of £260)
	Refine and use efficient written methods to multiply and divide HTU × U, TU × TU, U.t × U and HTU ÷ U	
	Find fractions using division (e.g. 1/100 of 5kg), and percentages of numbers and quantities (e.g. 10%, 5% and 15% of £80)	
Shape, space and measures Understanding shape	Identify, visualise and describe properties of rectangles, triangles, regular polygons and 3-D solids; use knowledge of properties to draw 2-D shapes, and to identify and draw nets of 3-D shapes	Describe, identify and visualise parallel and perpendicular edges or faces; use these properties to classify 2-D shapes and 3-D solids
	Read and plot coordinates in the first quadrant; recognise parallel and perpendicular lines in grids and shapes; use a set-square and ruler to draw shapes with perpendicular or parallel sides	Make and draw shapes with increasing accuracy and apply knowledge of their properties
	Complete patterns with up to two lines of symmetry; draw the position of a shape after a reflection or translation	**Visualise and draw on grids of different types where a shape will be after reflection, after translation, or after rotation through 90° or 180° about its centre or one of its vertices**
	Estimate, draw and measure acute and obtuse angles using an angle measurer or protractor to a suitable degree of accuracy; calculate angles in a straight line	Use coordinates in the first quadrant to draw, locate and complete shapes that meet given properties
		Estimate angles, and use a protractor to measure and draw them, on their own and in shapes; calculate angles in a triangle or around a point
Shape, space and measures Measuring	Read, choose, use and record standard metric units to estimate and measure length, weight and capacity to a suitable degree of accuracy (e.g. the nearest centimetre); convert larger to smaller units using decimals to one place (e.g. change 2.6kg to 2600g)	Select and use standard metric units of measure and convert between units using decimals to two places (e.g. change 2.75 litres to 2750ml, or vice versa)
	Interpret a reading that lies between two unnumbered divisions on a scale	Read and interpret scales on a range of measuring instruments, recognising that the measurement made is approximate and recording results to a required degree of accuracy; compare readings on different scales, for example when using different instruments
	Draw and measure lines to the nearest millimetre; measure and calculate the perimeter of regular and irregular polygons; use the formula for the area of a rectangle to calculate the rectangle's area	Calculate the perimeter and area of rectilinear shapes; estimate the area of an irregular shape by counting squares
	Read timetables and time using 24-hour clock notation; use a calendar to calculate time intervals	
Handling data	Describe the occurrence of familiar events using the language of chance or likelihood	Describe and predict outcomes from data using the language of chance or likelihood
	Answer a set of related questions by collecting, selecting and organising relevant data; draw conclusions, using ICT to present features, and identify further questions to ask	**Solve problems by collecting, selecting, processing, presenting and interpreting data, using ICT where appropriate; draw conclusions and identify further questions to ask**
	Construct frequency tables, pictograms and bar and line graphs to represent the frequencies of events and changes over time	Construct and interpret frequency tables, bar charts with grouped discrete data, and line graphs; interpret pie charts
	Find and interpret the mode of a set of data	Describe and interpret results and solutions to problems using the mode, range, median and mean

Answers

Level 3 – The Tricky Bits

Page 12 – Fractions

$\frac{6}{8}$ circled; $\frac{2}{8}$ not circled

Answers will vary e.g. $\frac{2}{8} = \frac{1}{4}$; $\frac{1}{3} = \frac{2}{6}$.

Page 13 – Classifying shapes

	Cone	Cylinder	Sphere	Cuboid	Triangular-based pyramid	Triangular prism
Number of faces	2	3	1	6	4	5
Number of edges	1	2	0	12	6	9
Number of vertices	1	0	0	8	4	6

Page 14 – Bar charts and pictograms

1) tuna mayonnaise 2) 7 3) 18

Page 15 – Decimal notation and negative numbers

1) 8 pounds, 26 pence 2) 56 pounds, 40 pence
3) 28 pounds, 4 pence
4) 780 pounds, 75 pence
5) 712 pounds, 97 pence

a) is colder

Number and algebra

Page 16 – Place value

1) a) $\frac{8}{100}$ b) 8 c) $\frac{8}{1000}$
d) $\frac{8}{100}$ e) 800

2) a) $3 + \frac{6}{10} + \frac{7}{100} + \frac{5}{1000}$ b) $40 + 5 + \frac{7}{100} + \frac{3}{1000}$
c) $60 + \frac{7}{1000}$

Page 17 – Place value

1) 5.66, 5.68, 5.86, 56.8, 58.6
2) 8.456, 8.546, 8.564, 8.645, 8.654
3) 4.7, 4.9, 7.3, 7.4, 7.5, 7.9
4) 3.36 km, 3.66 km, 3.663 km, 36.36 km, 36.6 km

Page 18 – Multiplying by 10 and 100

1) 760 2) 100 3) 54,300
4) 800 5) 18,000 6) 65

Page 19 – Dividing by 10 and 100

1) 840 2) 10 3) 50
4) 100 5) 90 6) 70

Page 20 – Addition

1) 9493 2) 16 639 3) 10 288
4) 8206

Page 21 – Subtraction

1) 1818 2) 5772 3) 5613
4) 6786

Page 22 – Short multiplication

1) 1944 2) 5080 3) 3470
4) 5635 5) 4452 6) 3411

Page 23 – Short division

1) 338 r1 2) 177 r1 3) 153 r2 4) 158 r5

Page 24 – Adding and subtracting decimals

1) 14.81 2) 123.5 m 3) £19.52
4) 29.17 5) 6.05 6) 27.65 g

Page 25 – Ratio and proportion

1) 8:6 or 4:3 (For every 4 red sweets there are 3 green sweets.)
2) 6:14 or $\frac{3}{7}$ (3 out of every 7 sweets are green.)

Page 26 – Checking your answers

1) 457 check 457 + 67 = 524
2) 40 check 40 × 4 = 160
3) 6987 check 6987 + 897 = 7884
4) 45 check 45 × 50 = 2250
5) 7557 Rough answer = 700 × 10 = 7000
6) 283 Rough answer 400 – 100 = 300
7) 26 Rough answer 460 ÷ 20 = 23

Page 27 – Checking your answers

1011
1) 9360 2) 1368 3) 6061
4) 4234 5) 2978 6) 4578
7) 3384 8) 417 9) 1722

Page 28 – Proportions of a whole

1) a) 23% b) 81% c) 10%
2) a) 77% b) 19% c) 90%

Page 29 – Important proportions

1) a) car b) 40

Page 30 – Number relationships

1) 1, 2, 3, 4, 6, 8, 12, 24
2) 1, 5, 7, 35
3) 1, 7, 49
4) 1, 2, 4, 8, 16, 32, 64

Square numbers to 100 are: 1, 4, 9, 16, 25, 36, 49, 64, 81, 100

Page 32 – Using coordinates
1 a) (3, 2) b) (3, 4) c) (1, 5)
2 a) bumper cars b) Fun House

Page 33 – Using coordinates
The coordinates are (5, 2).

Shape, space and measures

Page 34 – 2-D shapes
Answers will vary.

Page 35 – Properties of other 2-D shapes
Answers will vary.

Page 36 – 3-D shapes

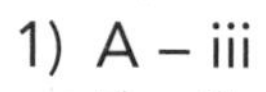

1) A – iii
B – ii
C – iv
D – i
E – v

2)

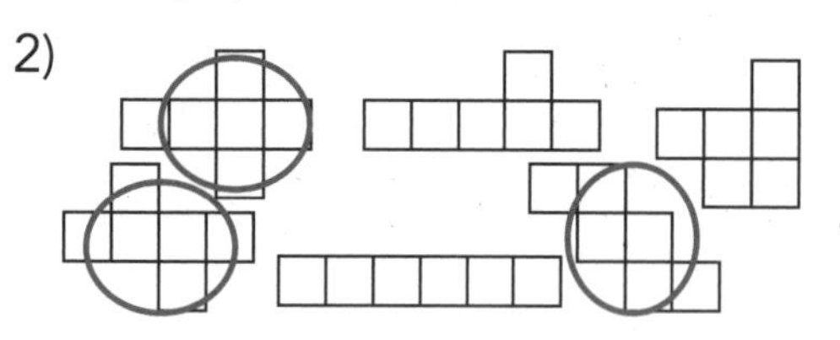

Page 37 – 3-D shapes
1) Needs 8 blocks to complete the cuboid
2) Needs 8 blocks to complete the cuboid

Page 38 – Angles
Order of angles: 30°, 56°, 100°, 134°, 170° – d, a, e, b, c
1) 40° 2) 62° 3) 137°

Page 40 – Moving 2-D shapes
a) b)

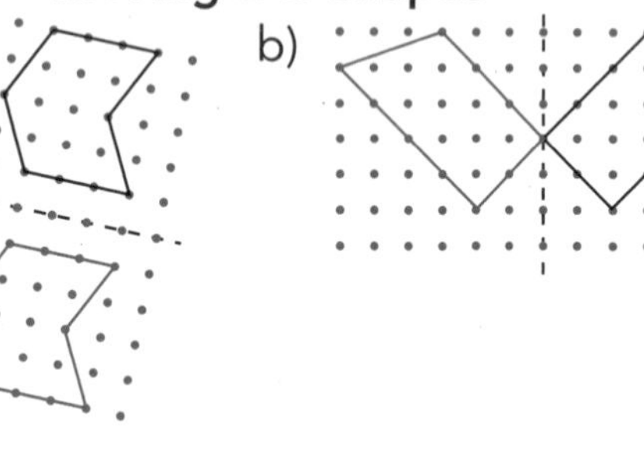

Page 41 – Moving 2-D shapes
1) a) 6 b) 4 c) 8
2)

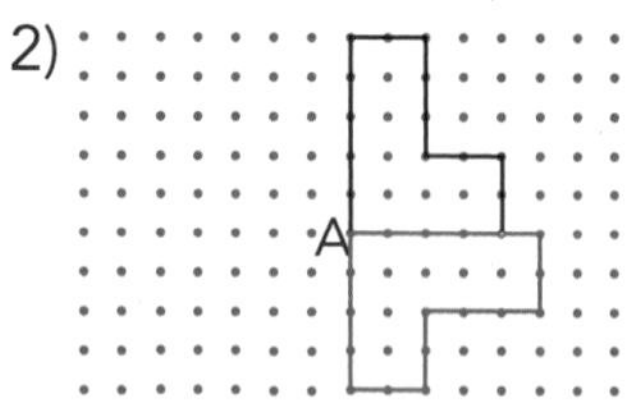

Page 42 – Perimeters of simple shapes
1) 13.2 cm 2) 18 cm

Page 43 – Areas of simple shapes
a) 9 cm^2 b) 5 cm^2 c) 10 cm^2

Page 44 – Measures
1) Your foot, DVD case
2) Glass of milk, can of cola, fish tank, paddling pool
3) Scales
4) Ruler
5) Answers will vary.

Page 45 – Reading scales
370 cm or 3.7 m

Page 47 – Time and timetables
1) 3 hours 35 mins 2) 4 hours 45 mins
3) 10:50 p.m. 4) 11:10 p.m.
5 a) 7:15 b) 8:10, 8:17
6 a) 8:55 a.m. or 5 to 9 b) 4:05 p.m. or 5 past 4
c) 4 hours and 10 minutes
7) 10:55 a.m. (or equivalent)

Handling data

Page 48 – Line graphs
1) a) March b) 1500
2) January and February
3) November
4) Description of event that would explain the increase (e.g. it was the summer holidays; there was a championship; they had a special offer/let people in free)
5) 3400 (allow 3350–3450 inclusive)

Page 49 – Line graphs
1) 5
2) Wednesday and Thursday
3) a) Upwards/increasing/getting higher
b) Friday

Page 50 – Grouping data
1) 2 2) 6 3) 6–10
4) 12 5) No

Page 52 – Finding the range and mode
Range = 49 Mode = 13

Using and applying mathematics

Page 55 – Number patterns
1) 20, 32. Rule is 'add 6'.
2) 6, 3. Rule is 'subtract 3'.
3) 57, 120, 141. Rule is 'add 21'.

Page 60 – Check problems by context
1) No – 20 runs would only hold 80 rabbits. 92 rabbits need 92 ÷ 4 = 23 runs.
2) No – in 40 minutes he would make 25 cubes / 21 cubes would take just over 33 minutes.